THE
OUTDOOR LEARNING ALMANAC
2025

Carol Murdoch

First Edition

Published by Carol Murdoch 2024
www.loveoutdoorlearning.com
Copyright © Carol Murdoch 2024

Carol Murdoch has asserted their right to be identified as the author of this Work in accordance with the Copyright, Designs and Patents Act 1988.

All rights reserved.

No part of this publication may be reproduced, stored in a retrieval system, or transmitted in any form or by any means, electronic, mechanical, photocopying, recording or otherwise, without the prior permission of the copyright owner.

All efforts have been made to ensure that dates within are correct, but some may be subject to cancellation or rearrangement after publication.

While every effort has been made to provide accurate and safe information in this book, the author and publisher cannot, under any circumstances, take responsibility for reaction to plants, incompatibility with certain health conditions, accidents or incidents while foraging, or discomfort illness, death caused by incorrect identification of wild foods. In addition, the author and publisher cannot, under any circumstances, take responsibility for accidents or incidents or discomfort illness, death caused through undertaking outdoor activities. Please seek professional medical/ foraging guidance where necessary, follow the Country Code and consider your own safety and actions.

CONTENTS

January	11
February	26
March	42
April	62
May	80
June	96
July	112
August	128
September	144
October	160
November	175
December	191
FIND OUT MORE	212

DEDICATION

To all the children, families, and educators who find joy in the outdoors and wonder in nature's smallest details. May this almanac inspire you to explore, connect, and learn from the world around you, wherever you may be.

For those who seek adventure in the wild, beauty in the everyday, and comfort in nature's cycles—this is for you.

And to the educators who, like me, may have once felt unsure about stepping outside to teach—know that the simplest connection with nature can be the most powerful.

Finally, heartfelt thanks needs to go to my amazing team, without whom this journey wouldn't have been possible—your passion and support have brought this project to life.

And to my husband, whose unwavering encouragement and belief in me make everything possible. Thank you for standing by my side through it all.

Thank you all for joining me on this journey.

WELCOME

Hello and welcome to our first Outdoor Learning Almanac. We've created this almanac to help families and educators make the most of the year ahead, offering inspiration to explore nature and incorporate outdoor learning into your daily life.

When I think back to my childhood, I remember summers spent at my Aunt and Uncle's down south, wandering through fields in search of berries—eating more than my fair share as my basket slowly filled. I remember watching the nights draw in and going for walks to spot meteors streaking across the sky. I can still recall the joy of growing my first broad bean plant and the excitement of teachers taking us outdoors to learn.

But as an educator, I initially struggled to fit outdoor learning into an already busy life and schedule. I felt unsure about taking children outdoors because I couldn't name every plant or animal—how could I teach outdoors with such gaps? Over time, through courses and experience, I realised two things. First, you don't need to know every plant and animal to connect meaningfully with nature (though I've certainly learned more!). More importantly, outdoor learning can be simple and supportive of everything you're already doing in the classroom—it's powerful without being complicated.

That's the foundation of this Outdoor Learning Almanac. 2025 has so much to offer, from full moons and meteor showers to Hedgehog Day and Nest Box Week. Each month brings new opportunities to get outside, and we've included space for 'could do' activities—suggestions to enrich your experience but without pressure. These ideas are here to inspire, not overwhelm, as you enjoy the outdoors.

Our theme for this year is connection. Each lesson and activity is designed to help you and your youngsters build a relationship with the land around you, whether you're in an urban environment or close to nature's abundance. Sometimes we forget to pay attention to the natural world, and this almanac encourages you to develop and strengthen that connection each month.

You'll also find tidal information throughout, based on data from Montrose, a central location on Scotland's east coast. Montrose was chosen because its moderate tidal variations offer a reliable baseline for coastal activities. Keep in mind that tides can vary by location, so check local tide tables if you're visiting a different coastline.

All the recipes, lessons, and activities have been thoroughly tried and tested by me. I'm Carol Murdoch, Director of Love Outdoor Learning. With a background in education (B.Ed.), an MSc in Learning for Sustainability, and years of experience as a Forest and Outdoor Learning Leader, I've crafted this almanac based on real-world experience. Every activity is practical, enjoyable, and designed to foster a deep connection with nature.

The content reflects Scotland's seasonal rhythms, but I recognise that seasonality can vary across the UK, particularly further north. While this almanac is based on Scotland's climate, I encourage you to adapt it to your local environment and embrace the unique seasonal changes in your area.

We've worked hard to ensure the dates, events, and information are as accurate as possible, but nature is ever-changing. Apologies for any discrepancies, and feel free to adjust based on your own observations and local conditions.

For those of you interested in foraging, remember to forage safely. Only pick what you can positively identify, and respect nature by leaving plenty for wildlife and other foragers. The natural world offers so much, but we must engage with it responsibly.

So, grab a cuppa, dive into the almanac, and see what January has in store. Use the 'could do' activities as inspiration to enjoy the outdoors—whether you're planning a seasonal recipe, exploring nature close to home, or following the phases of the moon. This *Outdoor Learning Almanac* is here to support you in making meaningful connections with the world around you.

Let's get started!

Carol

Hello,
January

01 JANUARY

As the clock strikes midnight, I feel a mix of melancholy for the past year and excitement for the one ahead. In Scotland, we're still wrapped in winter's darkness. Finding the motivation to step outside can be challenging, but it's always worthwhile.

When we venture outdoors, we start to notice the earth waking from its deep winter slumber. Snowdrops are often among the first signs of life, their delicate white blooms gently reminding us that nature is stirring even in the coldest months.

Legend has it that when Snow sought colour from the flowers, they turned away, thinking Snow too cold. Only the humble snowdrops offered their hue. In return, Snow allowed them to bloom through winter's chill. Now, snow and snowdrops are forever intertwined, each protecting the other.

Though January may feel like the darkest month, it's also the perfect time to embrace winter's serene beauty. Wrapping up warm and stepping outside, even briefly, can lift your spirits and connect you with nature's slow, steady awakening.

01 THE MONTH

8th (to 19th Feb)	Bug School Birdwatch
10th	House Plant Appreciation day
11th	Jump in a Puddle Day
17th	Big Energy Saving Week
18th	Winnie the Pooh Day
19th	Popcorn Day
	World Religion Day
20th	Penguin Day
21st	Squirrel Appreciation Day
23rd	Handwriting Day
24th	International Day of Education
25th	Burns Night
27th	Storytelling Week
29th	Chinese New Year

Could Do This Month...

♡ _____
♡ _____
♡ _____
♡ _____
♡ _____
♡ _____
♡ _____

01 GARDENING

January may feel like a harsh time to start gardening, with little hands in cold soil, but it's the perfect month for planning. While the ground is still frosty, you can get ahead by sowing seeds indoors, especially those that need a longer growing season. Peppers and chillies are a great choice to start in seed trays or small pots on a sunny windowsill or heated propagator. This early start ensures stronger plants when it's time to transplant them.

Out in the veg garden, a bit of tidying can go a long way. Clear away dead plant matter, pull up weeds, and if the soil is workable, add organic compost or manure to enrich it for the spring. Why not plan your garden layout—consider crop rotation and think about what worked well last year to improve this year's yield.

If you have any leeks or turnips still in the ground, January is a perfect time to harvest them. This is also a great time to connect with your local allotment or community garden. They're excellent resources for advice, seeds, and potential support, such as watering during the school holidays.

01 NIGHT SKY

Quadrantids Meteor Shower - January 3 - 4, 2025
The Quadrantids are expected to be the highlight of the month, with the peak occurring in the early hours of January 3rd. This meteor shower can produce up to 120 meteors per hour under optimal conditions.

5th - Mars, Jupiter, the moon, Saturn and Venus - January 5, 2025
You will be able to see all at the same time above the horizon around 18:40 between northeast and southwest.

The Moon - January 13, 2025
The Full Moon in January, known as the "Wolf Moon," will dominate the night sky.

Mars - January 16, 2025
This will be the highest and brightest Mars will be all year.

The Moon Phases

First Quarter	6th January
Full Moon	13th January
Last Quarter	21st January
New Moon	29th January

01 WILDLIFE

As winter gradually eases its grip, Mother Nature begins to stir. With even a slight rise in temperature, you might notice frogs emerging from their winter hiding spots. Listen closely at dusk, and you may catch the sound of their croaking calls.

January is an excellent time to observe ducks, especially as they start their mating rituals. Male Goldeneyes will perform an impressive display, throwing their heads back and whistling loudly while frantically kicking their feet—a truly spectacular sight!

Though many birds quieten down during the winter, robins are an exception. They intensify their song, making this a great time to tune in to their calls. Pay attention to their distinctive melodic notes, whistles, trills, and burbles, particularly in the early morning.
With the trees bare, red squirrels become easier to spot. They don't hibernate but do become less active during winter. Scotland is home to around 121,000 red squirrels, with notable populations in Aberdeenshire and Tayside.

Red deer, too, come down from their usual higher ground and are more likely to be seen as they move to lower elevations in search of food.

01   GARDEN LIFE

Blackthorn blossom is one of the first signs of spring, releasing its sweet, almond-like fragrance, reminiscent of a warm snowfall. Queen bees, having rested through the winter, also begin to emerge, searching for early pollen and a suitable place to lay their eggs. Meanwhile, early-nesting birds like ravens are busy building their nests, preparing for the new life that's just around the corner.

Even in January, despite the chill, there's interesting wildlife to spot in your garden in Scotland. Common birds such as robins, blackbirds, blue tits, and great tits remain active, especially if you offer bird feeders. You might also see goldfinches, sparrows, and chaffinches foraging for seeds and berries.

Although most hedgehogs hibernate, some may wake during warmer spells to search for food. If your garden has hedgehog-friendly spots like leaf piles, you might catch a glimpse of one on a mild evening.
Additionally, some insects, like queen bumblebees and ladybirds, may appear on milder days, emerging from their winter hideouts. By providing food, water, and shelter, you can encourage these creatures to visit even during the colder months.

01 COOKING

Bannock Bread
Ingredients:
2 cups plain flour
1 tsp baking powder
1/2 tsp salt
1/2 cup water (adjust as needed)
Optional: butter, honey, or jam for serving

Instructions:
1. In a large bowl, mix together the flour, baking powder, and salt. Slowly add the water to the dry ingredients. Start with half a cup and mix with your hands or a spoon until a dough forms. Add more water if needed, but keep the dough firm, not sticky.
2. Once combined, knead the dough for about 2-3 minutes until it's smooth. It should hold its shape but still be soft and easy to handle.
3. Divide the dough into small balls (about the size of a golf ball). Flatten each ball into a patty shape, about 1 cm thick.

   On a stick: Skewer the flattened dough onto a stick, wrapping it around tightly. Hold it over the fire, turning regularly to cook evenly.

   On a hot stone or pan: Place the dough patties directly on a heated stone or in a cast-iron skillet over the fire. Cook for about 5-10 minutes on each side, or until golden brown and cooked through.

01 THE SEA

Date	HEIGHTS ABOVE CHART DATUM							
	High Water				Low Water			
	Morning		Afternoon		Morning		Afternoon	
	Time	m	Time	m	Time	m	Time	m
1 W	02 54	4.6	14 57	4.8	08 27	1.5	20 56	1.1
2 TH	03 33	4.6	15 34	4.8	09 07	1.4	21 38	1.1
3 F	04 16	4.6	16 14	4.8	09 48	1.5	22 22	1.0
4 SA	05 00	4.5	16 57	4.8	10 31	1.5	23 09	1.1
5 **SU**	05 47	4.4	17 44	4.7	11 17	1.6	23 59	1.2
6 M ☽	06 40	4.3	18 38	4.6			12 08	1.8
7 TU	07 38	4.1	19 40	4.5	00 55	1.3	13 09	1.9
8 W	08 42	4.1	20 49	4.3	01 56	1.5	14 18	2.0
9 TH	09 51	4.1	22 05	4.3	03 02	1.6	15 32	2.0
10 F	11 00	4.2	23 22	4.4	04 15	1.7	16 48	1.8
11 SA			12 02	4.4	05 24	1.7	17 54	1.6
12 **SU**	00 29	4.5	12 55	4.6	06 20	1.6	18 48	1.3
13 M ○	01 25	4.6	13 41	4.7	07 09	1.5	19 38	1.1
14 TU	02 14	4.7	14 23	4.8	07 52	1.5	20 22	1.0
15 W	02 59	4.7	15 03	4.9	08 32	1.5	21 05	0.9
16 TH	03 39	4.6	15 40	4.9	09 09	1.5	21 43	1.0
17 F	04 18	4.5	16 18	4.8	09 44	1.5	22 21	1.1
18 SA	04 54	4.4	16 53	4.7	10 18	1.6	22 56	1.2
19 **SU**	05 31	4.2	17 31	4.5	10 52	1.7	23 34	1.4
20 M	06 09	4.0	18 11	4.3	11 29	1.9		
21 TU ☾	06 52	3.9	18 58	4.1	00 14	1.6	12 11	2.1
22 W	07 43	3.7	19 56	3.9	01 01	1.9	13 07	2.3
23 TH	08 43	3.7	21 05	3.7	01 58	2.1	14 21	2.4
24 F	09 53	3.7	22 27	3.7	03 06	2.2	15 46	2.4
25 SA	11 05	3.8	23 41	3.8	04 23	2.2	17 06	2.2
26 **SU**			12 03	4.0	05 26	2.1	17 59	1.9
27 M	00 37	4.0	12 50	4.3	06 14	1.9	18 41	1.6
28 TU	01 21	4.3	13 29	4.5	06 55	1.7	19 22	1.3
29 W ●	02 01	4.5	14 05	4.7	07 35	1.4	20 02	1.0
30 TH	02 41	4.7	14 42	4.9	08 14	1.3	20 43	0.8
31 F	03 19	4.8	15 19	5.1	08 53	1.1	21 23	0.7

Time Zone UT(GMT)

01   SCAVENGER

 Brown leaf

 Sparkles in the air

 Snow

 Berries

 Ice

 Pine Cone

 Robin

 Your Breath

 Geese Migrating

 Leafless Tree

 Pine Needles

 Animal Tracks

 Cold Morning

 Clear Moon

 Windy Trees

 Evergreen Leaf

PINECONE FEEDERS

Objective:
Create a simple pinecone feeder to attract and feed bird birds in your garden.

What You'll Need:
Large pinecone
Peanut butter (or a nut-free alternative like sunflower seed butter)
Birdseed mix
String or twine (30-40 cm)
Butter knife or spoon

Instructions:
1. Find a large, open pinecone. If it's closed, bake it at a low temperature (200°F or 93°C) for 30 minutes to open it up, then let it cool completely.
2. Cut a piece of string or twine about 30-40 cm long. Tie it securely around the top of the pinecone, creating a loop for hanging.
3. Use a butter knife, spoon, or your fingers to spread a thick layer of peanut butter (or nut-free alternative) all over the pinecone, getting it into all the crevices.
4. Pour birdseed mix onto a plate or dish. Roll the peanut butter-covered pinecone in the birdseed

until fully coated. Press birdseed into the peanut butter to help it stick.
5. Choose a tree branch or bird feeder hook to hang your pinecone bird feeder. Ensure it's securely fastened and in a spot visible to birds but safe from predators.
6. Check the feeder regularly, refilling it with peanut butter and birdseed as needed. Replace the pinecone if it becomes too worn out.

Why It's Great:
- Easy and fun way to feed local birds.
- Encourages outdoor exploration and nature observation.
- Simple craft suitable for all ages.

Remember:
- Choose a safe location away from predators.
- Make multiple feeders to attract a variety of birds.
- Keep an eye on the feeder and refill it when necessary.

NATURAL LETTERS

Objective:

Help children explore the natural world while learning about letters. By using natural materials like sticks, leaves, and rocks, children will create letters of the alphabet, developing creativity, fine motor skills, and environmental awareness.

What You'll Need:

Loose natural materials (sticks, leaves, rocks, etc.)
Outdoor space or a collection of natural materials indoors
Optional: Paper or a surface for creating letters, glue or tape for securing materials

Instructions:

1. Start by discussing how we can use materials found in nature to be creative. Explain that just as we can write letters on paper, we can also use things like sticks and leaves to make letters outside.
2. Take the children outdoors or provide them with natural materials inside. Encourage them to gather items like sticks, stones, leaves, and other found objects.

3. Demonstrate how to form a letter using these natural materials. Let children create their own letters of the alphabet using the collected materials. They can work independently or in small groups.
4. Once the letters are made, gather everyone to display their creations. Go through each letter, reinforcing letter recognition and discussing how the natural materials were used to form them.

Why It's Great:
- Hands-On Learning: Encourages creativity and letter recognition through a tactile, nature-based activity.
- Flexible: Can be done indoors or outdoors, using materials available in the environment.
- Environmental Awareness: Fosters a connection to nature while exploring letters.

Remember:
- It's not about perfection but about creativity.
- Let the children explore different ways to form their letters. Some might use only rocks, while others might combine sticks and leaves. Each letter can look unique, just like the materials they're made from.

NOTES

Hello, February

02 FEBRUARY

As February settles in, there's a quiet shift in the air. Though the days remain short and cold, there's a softening that hints spring is approaching. Mornings in Scotland begin to brighten, tempting us to step outside despite the lingering chill.

Nature's changes are subtle but noticeable. Crocuses start to push through the frost, adding vibrant splashes of colour to the winter landscape.

February also brings a touch of Scottish wisdom: "If Candlemas Day is fair and bright, winter will have another flight; but if it brings cloud and rain, winter is gone and will not come again." This old saying suggests that clear weather may mean winter lingers a bit longer, while cloudy days signal the approach of spring.

Despite the cold, stepping outside reveals the first signs of spring. A brisk walk-through woodlands or along hedgerows can uncover new life, from snowdrops to crocuses, and the occasional early bee or squirrel. The crisp air is invigorating, and a short outdoor adventure can lift your spirits and reconnect you with nature's emerging rhythms. So, wrap up warm and enjoy the subtle beauty of February.

02 THE MONTH

LGBTQ+ Month
Build Your Self Esteem Month

5th	Children's Mental Health Week
7th	NSPCC Number Day
11th	International Day of Women and Girls in Science
14th	Valentines Day
14th	Nest Box Week
17th	Random Acts of Kindness Day
26th	Tell a Fairytale Day
27th	Polar Bear Day
27th	Fairtrade Fortnight
28th (to 30th Mar)	Ramadan

Could Do This Month...

♡ _____
♡ _____
♡ _____
♡ _____
♡ _____
♡ _____
♡ _____

02 GARDENING

February is when I start thinking about deep cleaning my polytunnel, greenhouse and garden equipment. The best part is it is active so keeps me warm and the washing up can be completed indoors!

Terra cotta and clay pots
Use a stiff wire brush to remove loose soil and mineral deposits. You can also soak the pots in a solution of four parts water and one part vinegar for up to 30 minutes. After cleaning, rinse the pots thoroughly and let them air dry for at least 48 hours before using or storing them.

Plastic or varnished ceramic pots
Use hot water, gentle washing up liquid, and a scrubbing brush to clean the inside and outside of the pot. Pay special attention to nooks and crannies.

Fabric pots
If the pots are clean, you can let them dry, fold, and store them. If they are stained, you can wash them in the washing machine or soak them in a bucket with laundry detergent. Rinse thoroughly and air dry.

And, if there are still leeks and turnips out there, I can harvest some more!

02 NIGHT SKY

Full Moon – February 12, 2025

This February, we'll experience the Full Moon, often called the "Snow Moon." It will light up the winter skies, adding a soft, luminous glow to the cold, crisp nights. This full moon provides a beautiful chance to appreciate the serene beauty of the winter landscape under its gentle light.

Venus at Its Highest – February 7-16, 2025

Venus, known as the "Evening Star," will reach its highest point in the sky from February 7th to 16th. Beginning its ascent on the 7th, it will steadily brighten, with its peak brilliance occurring on the 16th. After sunset, Venus will shine brightly, offering a stunning celestial view that's perfect for stargazers eager to catch a glimpse of our neighbouring planet in all its splendour.

The Moon Phases

First Quarter	5th February
Full Moon	12th February
Last Quarter	20th February
New Moon	28th February

02 WILDLIFE

In February, nature is waking up from its winter rest. Squirrels become more active, darting through the trees as they search for hidden food stores. If you're fortunate, you might catch the early signs of courtship as they prepare for the breeding season. Despite the cold nights, the haunting hoots of owls echo through the dark woods, signalling their territorial calls as they search for mates.

This month is also an excellent time for birdwatching. Look out for wintering birds like whooper swans, barnacle geese, and pink-footed geese, which can often be seen in the many lochs and estuaries across Scotland.

Along the coastlines, especially in regions like the Firth of Forth, Orkney, and the Hebrides, you might spot grey and common seals. February is a great time to observe these seals as they haul out on the shores.

Though otters can be elusive, February provides a good opportunity to spot them. They are often more active during daylight hours as they forage for food in quieter areas of rivers, lochs, and along the coast.

02 GARDEN LIFE

In February, trees start their subtle preparation for spring. The hazel is one of the first to show signs of life, with its long catkins—often called 'lambs' tails'—dangling delicately from the branches. These pale yellow clusters sway gently in the wind, marking the start of the pollination season and offering a crucial early food source for bees as they begin to emerge from their winter rest.

If you look closely in the hedgerows, you might spot the first leaves of wild garlic pushing through the leaf litter. Although it's too early for them to flower, their vibrant green leaves hint at the bounty that will soon fill the woods with their distinctive, garlicky aroma.

Your garden in Scotland can still be a lively spot for wildlife in February. Garden birds like robins, blackbirds, and finches remain frequent visitors to feeders, and you might also see long-tailed tits and starlings searching for food.

Though hedgehogs are mostly in hibernation, a warm spell might wake them briefly. Keeping garden shelters available ensures they have a safe place to retreat if they do wake. Your garden plays a crucial role in supporting wildlife during this transition from winter to spring.

02   FORAGING

Scots Pine Needle

To identify Scots pine for foraging, start by looking at its needles, cones, and overall shape. Scots pine needles grow in pairs, are bluish-green, and measure about 3-7 cm in length. These needles are soft, flexible, and cylindrical, making them distinct from the sharper, more rigid needles of other conifers like spruce.

Scots pine also produces long, woody cones that hang from the branches, which is another key feature. The bark of mature Scots pine is reddish-brown and has a distinctive flaky, scaly texture. The overall shape of the tree is typically tall and conical, with widely spaced branches that give it an airy, open appearance.

When foraging for Scots pine needles, make sure to pick only fresh, green needles. Always forage sustainably by taking small amounts from several trees, rather than stripping one tree entirely. These features—paired needles, distinctive cones, and flaky bark—make Scots pine relatively easy to identify in the wild.

02   COOKING

Pine Needle Tea

To make pine needle tea, begin by identifying and collecting fresh, green pine needles from a true pine tree, such as a Scots pine. Be careful to avoid toxic trees like yew. The needles should have a fresh, piney smell. Once you've gathered a small handful, rinse the needles thoroughly to remove any dirt or debris. After rinsing, cut the needles into small pieces, about 1 to 2 centimetres in length, to release more flavour and nutrients.

Next, bring two cups of water to a boil over a campfire or on a stove. Once the water is boiling, remove it from the heat and add the chopped pine needles. Cover the pot or cup to let the tea steep, as this helps preserve the aromatic oils and flavour. Allow the pine needles to steep in the hot water for around 10 minutes. You'll notice the water changing to a light yellow or greenish colour during this time.

After the tea has steeped, strain it into a cup to remove the pine needles. If you like, you can add a bit of honey or a squeeze of lemon to enhance the flavour, though the tea already has a natural, slightly citrusy taste. Finally, enjoy your warm, fragrant pine needle tea, perfect for an outdoor adventure or cosy campfire moment.

02 THE SEA

Date	High Water Morning Time	m	High Water Afternoon Time	m	Low Water Morning Time	m	Low Water Afternoon Time	m
1 SA	03 59	4.9	15 58	5.2	09 32	1.1	22 05	0.6
2 **SU**	04 39	4.8	16 38	5.1	10 11	1.2	22 46	0.7
3 M	05 21	4.6	17 22	5.0	10 52	1.3	23 31	0.9
4 TU	06 07	4.4	18 11	4.8	11 38	1.5		
5 W ☽	07 01	4.2	19 11	4.5	00 22	1.2	12 34	1.7
6 TH	08 05	4.0	20 26	4.2	01 20	1.6	13 44	1.9
7 F	09 20	3.9	21 55	4.0	02 32	1.9	15 11	2.0
8 SA	10 43	3.9	23 26	4.1	04 03	2.0	16 47	1.9
9 **SU**	11 56	4.1			05 23	2.0	17 55	1.6
10 M	00 36	4.2	12 51	4.4	06 19	1.8	18 47	1.3
11 TU	01 28	4.4	13 35	4.6	07 03	1.6	19 32	1.1
12 W ○	02 09	4.5	14 12	4.8	07 41	1.5	20 10	0.9
13 TH	02 45	4.6	14 47	4.9	08 15	1.4	20 46	0.8
14 F	03 17	4.6	15 19	4.9	08 48	1.3	21 18	0.8
15 SA	03 48	4.5	15 51	4.9	09 18	1.3	21 48	0.9
16 **SU**	04 19	4.4	16 22	4.7	09 46	1.3	22 19	1.1
17 M	04 49	4.3	16 53	4.6	10 16	1.4	22 49	1.3
18 TU	05 21	4.2	17 28	4.4	10 47	1.6	23 22	1.5
19 W	05 56	4.0	18 08	4.1	11 23	1.8		
20 TH ☾	06 40	3.8	19 01	3.8	00 00	1.8	12 06	2.0
21 F	07 37	3.6	20 12	3.6	00 50	2.1	13 10	2.3
22 SA	08 51	3.5	21 40	3.5	02 02	2.3	14 46	2.4
23 **SU**	10 15	3.6	23 14	3.7	03 38	2.4	16 33	2.2
24 M	11 32	3.8			05 04	2.2	17 37	1.9
25 TU	00 17	3.9	12 25	4.1	05 55	1.9	18 21	1.5
26 W	01 02	4.3	13 06	4.5	06 37	1.6	19 02	1.1
27 TH	01 42	4.6	13 44	4.8	07 15	1.3	19 41	0.7
28 F ●	02 19	4.8	14 20	5.1	07 54	1.0	20 21	0.5

Time Zone UT(GMT)

35

02 SCAVENGER

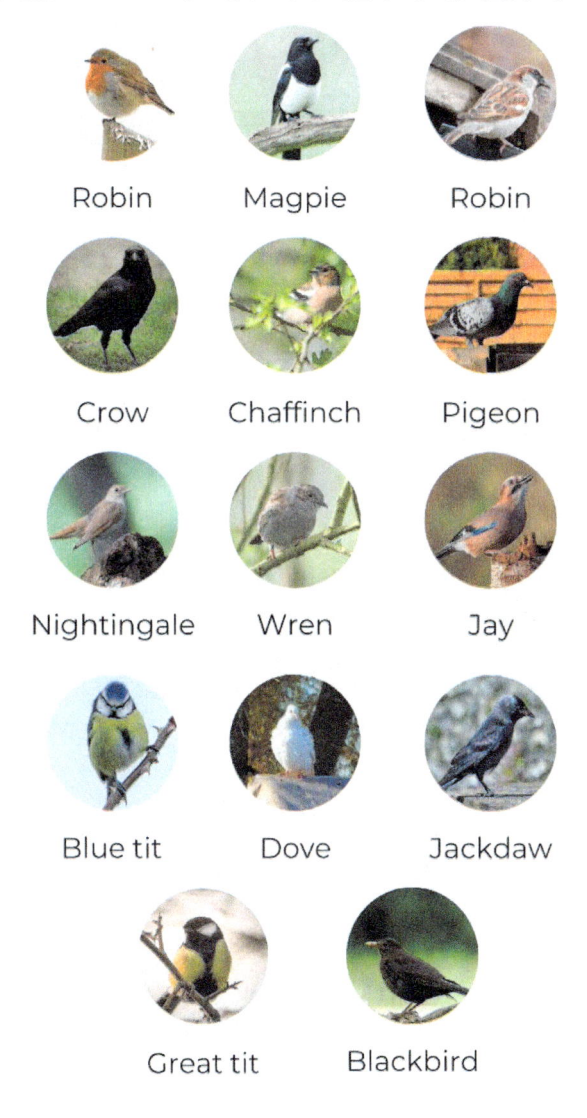

Robin	Magpie	Robin
Crow	Chaffinch	Pigeon
Nightingale	Wren	Jay
Blue tit	Dove	Jackdaw
Great tit	Blackbird	

LISTEN OUTDOORS

Objective:
Help children enhance their listening skills by tuning into the sounds of nature and creating a sound map to represent their experience.

What You'll Need:
Paper
Drawing materials (coloured pencils, crayons, or markers)
Optional: Clipboards for outdoor use

Instructions:
1. Gather the children in a quiet outdoor space and explain they'll be focusing on nature's sounds, emphasising the importance of listening carefully.

2. Give each child paper and drawing materials. Ask them to sit quietly, close their eyes, and listen. After a few moments, have them draw symbols or shapes to represent the sounds they hear, creating a "sound map."

3. Once finished, gather in a circle to share and discuss their sound maps. Ask questions like, "Did anything surprise you?" and "What sounds did you hear the most?" Encourage them to keep exploring and listening for new sounds.

Why It's Great:
- Encourages focus on different sounds and deepens awareness of the environment.
- Allows for imaginative expression through sound mapping, turning sounds into symbols and pictures.
- Can be adapted to be as simple or complex as needed.

Remember:
- Listening to nature is a simple but powerful way to connect with the environment.
- Whether for older or younger children, this activity helps develop their observation and creative skills while fostering a sense of peace and awareness in outdoor spaces.

FAIRY HOMES

Objective:
Encourage children to engage with nature by building mini twig wigwams, fostering creativity, fine motor skills, and an appreciation for the natural environment.

What You'll Need:
Twigs (finger thickness)
Twine or wool
Optional: natural decorations (leaves, moss, small sticks)

Instructions:
1. Gather children outdoors and explain they'll be building mini twig wigwams for fairies or creatures using natural materials.
2. Have them collect a small handful of twigs, ensuring they do so responsibly without harming the environment.
3. Help them choose a good spot, considering sunlight, flat ground, and access to materials.
4. Instruct them to push twigs into the ground in a circular pattern to form the base, then secure the tops with twine or wool.
5. Encourage creativity by decorating the wigwams with leaves, moss, and small sticks.

6. After finishing, ask the children to share their wigwams and reflect on the building process.

Why It's Great:
- Hands-on activity that builds fine motor skills and engages children with nature.
- Fosters creativity in design and decoration.

Remember:
This activity promotes teamwork, creativity, and practical skills, making it suitable for a variety of age groups.

ial-2.0/), which permits use, sharing, adaptation, distribution and reproduction in any medium or format, as long as you give appropriate credit to the original author(s) and the source, provide a link to the Creative Commons licence, and indicate if changes were made. The images or other third party material in this article are included in the article's Creative Commons licence, unless indicated otherwise in a credit line to the material. If material is not included in the article's Creative Commons licence and your intended use is not permitted by statutory regulation or exceeds the permitted use, you will need to obtain permission directly from the copyright holder. To view a copy of this licence, visit http://creativecommons.org/licenses/by-nc/4.0/.

NOTES

Hello,
March

03 MARCH

As March arrives, the landscape begins to transform, bringing a sense of renewal with it. The days grow noticeably longer, and the sharp edge of winter starts to soften. While the wind may still nip, there's an unmistakable feeling that spring is just around the corner. The outdoors beckons with the promise of new life, making it a perfect time to step outside.

March also brings with it an old Scottish saying: "If March comes in like a lion, it will go out like a lamb." This folk wisdom suggests that a stormy start to the month will give way to calmer, milder weather by the end. Whether this old tale holds true or not, it's a reminder of the transitional nature of the season.

As nature shakes off winter's hold, heading outside in March will reward you with the first signs of spring—early blooms, the lively chatter of birds, and the soothing sound of water flowing with new life. The brisk, early spring air feels fresh and invigorating, lifting your spirits as you witness nature's steady progression toward brighter days. So wrap up warmly and embrace the outdoors—spring is waiting for you.

03 THE MONTH

1st	St David's Day
2nd	Old Stuff Day
3rd	World Wildlife Day
	World Hearing Day
4th	Shrove Tuesday
5th	Ash Wednesday
6th	World Book Day
7th	British Science Week
12th	Plant a Flower Day
14th	Holi
17th	St Patrick's Day
20th	World Frog Day
	Spring Equinox
	International Day of Happiness
21st	World Poetry Day
21st	GB Spring Clean
23rd	World Meteorological Day
28th	Skipping Day

Could Do This Month...

♡ _____
♡ _____
♡ _____
♡ _____

03 GARDENING

By March, daffodils take centre stage with their golden heads nodding in the breeze, brightening the still-muted landscape. Primroses join in, scattering soft yellow flowers across woodland floors and hedgerows, adding a delicate touch of colour. The vibrant purple-blue crocuses further enhance the scene, signalling that winter is slowly retreating.

In the garden, as the lighter days return, It's time to start sowing in the greenhouse. I'm planning to grow lettuce, spinach, and squash (still working on perfecting that!). I loved the Tumbling Toms tomatoes from 2024—they're perfect for vertical planters in small spaces. I'll also be sowing peas (great as microgreens), leeks, sprouts, kohlrabi, and cauliflower.

While there isn't much to harvest yet, my microgreens are thriving. They're packed with nutrients and perfect for adding to sandwiches, wraps, or simply as a side. The early spring growth feels invigorating, and the garden is starting to come alive again.

03 NIGHT SKY

Vernal Equinox – March 20, 2025
On this date, day and night are nearly equal in length as the sun sits directly above the equator. This marks the official start of spring and the point where the balance of daylight and darkness shifts towards longer days.

Full Moon – March 14, 2025
The Full Moon will occur at 06:55 GMT and is often called the "Worm Moon." This name reflects the time when the ground starts to soften, allowing earthworms to emerge, heralding the arrival of spring.

Partial Solar Eclipse – March 29, 2025
A partial solar eclipse will be visible, covering about 30% of the sun. It starts around 10:10 GMT, with maximum coverage occurring at 11:00 GMT. Remember to never look directly at the sun without proper protection, as this can cause serious eye damage.

The Moon Phases
First Quarter	6TH March
Full Moon	14th March
Last Quarter	22nd March
New Moon	29th March

03   WILDLIFE

March is a vibrant month for birdlife, as the days grow longer, and dawn arrives with a symphony of birdsong. Blackbirds, robins, and song thrushes greet the morning with their melodious tunes. Many birds are busy building their nests. Keep an eye on the skies, and you may even see the first swallows and sand martins returning from their long migration, their graceful flight symbolising renewal and the changing season.

This month also brings the reappearance of animals that have been hidden away during winter. You might also notice increased activity from badgers and foxes, with foxes often seen foraging in the early morning or evening light. In ponds and streams, clusters of frogspawn begin to appear, marking the next stage in the life cycle.

Among the most charming sights in March is the return of the puffin to their breeding colonies. Their bright colours and distinctive beaks make them one of the most jolly-looking birds you can find. Not far behind, Ospreys also start returning to Scotland this month after wintering in Africa. Look for these magnificent birds near large lochs and rivers, where they'll set up nests and begin fishing for their young.

03 GARDEN LIFE

In March, your garden in Scotland truly begins to awaken as spring draws near. Birds like robins, blackbirds, and blue tits can be seen darting around, busily collecting twigs, moss, and leaves to build their nests. Bird boxes and hedges become hives of activity as they prepare for the nesting season. This increased bird presence brings energy to the garden, and you may hear their early morning calls more frequently as they establish territories and communicate with mates.

As temperatures gradually rise, the garden's first flowers begin to bloom, adding splashes of colour to the still-chilly landscape. Crocuses and primroses, some of the earliest flowers to bloom, attract the attention of bumblebees and other early pollinators. On sunny days, these hardy bees emerge from hibernation to visit the blooms, gathering nectar and pollen to feed their new colonies. Their presence is a clear sign that spring is on its way.

Garden ponds also come alive in March, with frogs and toads returning to their breeding grounds. The sound of croaking frogs is a sure indication of the busy breeding season ahead. Frogs and toads lay their eggs in clusters, and soon, your pond may be filled with tadpoles, signalling the start of new life.

03 FORAGING

Wild Garlic

To identify wild garlic (Allium ursinum) for foraging, look for its broad, green leaves that grow in damp, shady woodlands, often near streams. The leaves are smooth, lance-shaped, and can grow up to 25 cm long. One of the easiest ways to confirm its wild garlic is by crushing a leaf between your fingers—if it smells strongly of garlic, you've found the right plant.

In spring, wild garlic produces small white star-shaped flowers that grow in clusters. These flowers are edible too, but the leaves are often foraged before the plant flowers for the best flavour. Wild garlic typically grows in dense patches and spreads quickly in its ideal environment.

When foraging, avoid confusing wild garlic with plants like lily of the valley, which has similar-looking leaves but is toxic. Always use the strong garlic scent to verify your find. Harvest only what you need, ensuring there's enough left for the plant to continue growing and spreading. Wild garlic is a versatile, delicious ingredient that can be used in pesto, soups, or salads.

03 COOKING

Wild Garlic Butter

Ingredients:
100g butter, softened
A handful of wild garlic leaves, finely chopped
A pinch of salt

Instructions:
1. Chop the wild garlic: Wash and dry the wild garlic leaves, then chop them finely.
2. Mix with butter: In a bowl, mix the softened butter with the chopped wild garlic and a pinch of salt until well combined.
3. Shape and chill: Spoon the mixture onto cling film or parchment paper. Roll it into a log shape and twist the ends to seal. Place it in the fridge to firm up for about 30 minutes.
Serve: Once chilled, slice and use as a spread on bread, melted over vegetables, or added to dishes for extra flavour.
This wild garlic butter is a versatile and flavourful addition to many meals!

03 THE SEA

Date	\multicolumn{4}{c|}{High Water}	\multicolumn{4}{c|}{Low Water}
	\multicolumn{2}{c|}{Morning}	\multicolumn{2}{c|}{Afternoon}	\multicolumn{2}{c|}{Morning}	\multicolumn{2}{c|}{Afternoon}
	Time	m	Time	m	Time	m	Time	m
1 SA	02 57	5.0	14 58	5.3	08 31	0.9	21 01	0.3
2 SU	03 34	5.0	15 36	5.3	09 10	0.8	21 40	0.4
3 M	04 13	4.9	16 18	5.3	09 48	0.8	22 21	0.6
4 TU	04 53	4.7	17 02	5.0	10 29	1.0	23 03	0.9
5 W	05 37	4.4	17 52	4.7	11 15	1.2	23 52	1.4
6 TH ☽	06 29	4.1	18 56	4.3			12 11	1.5
7 F	07 35	3.9	20 18	3.9	00 52	1.8	13 27	1.8
8 SA	08 56	3.7	21 58	3.8	02 14	2.2	15 08	1.9
9 SU	10 31	3.8	23 32	3.9	04 04	2.2	16 48	1.7
10 M	11 47	4.0			05 19	2.1	17 49	1.4
11 TU	00 33	4.1	12 39	4.3	06 09	1.8	18 35	1.2
12 W	01 17	4.3	13 19	4.5	06 48	1.6	19 14	1.0
13 TH	01 52	4.4	13 54	4.7	07 21	1.4	19 47	0.9
14 F ○	02 21	4.5	14 24	4.8	07 52	1.2	20 18	0.8
15 SA	02 49	4.6	14 54	4.8	08 21	1.1	20 47	0.8
16 SU	03 16	4.5	15 22	4.8	08 50	1.1	21 15	0.9
17 M	03 44	4.5	15 52	4.7	09 17	1.2	21 42	1.1
18 TU	04 12	4.4	16 23	4.5	09 45	1.3	22 10	1.3
19 W	04 41	4.3	16 57	4.3	10 15	1.4	22 40	1.5
20 TH	05 14	4.1	17 35	4.1	10 48	1.6	23 15	1.8
21 F	05 52	3.9	18 25	3.8	11 30	1.8		
22 SA ☾	06 44	3.7	19 37	3.5	00 00	2.1	12 30	2.1
23 SU	08 02	3.5	21 05	3.5	01 13	2.3	14 04	2.2
24 M	09 28	3.5	22 40	3.6	03 00	2.4	15 53	2.1
25 TU	10 51	3.7	23 48	4.0	04 33	2.2	17 05	1.7
26 W	11 51	4.1			05 27	1.8	17 52	1.3
27 TH	00 35	4.3	12 36	4.5	06 10	1.5	18 33	0.9
28 F	01 14	4.6	13 15	4.8	06 49	1.2	19 14	0.5
29 SA ●	01 52	4.9	13 55	5.2	07 28	0.9	19 54	0.3
30 SU	02 29	5.0	14 34	5.3	08 06	0.7	20 34	0.3
31 M	03 08	5.1	15 15	5.4	08 46	0.6	21 15	0.4

Time Zone UT(GMT)

03   SCAVENGER

A matchbox scavenger hunt is a fun, creative activity that encourages exploration. Participants search for small items that fit inside a matchbox. Here's how to organise it:

What You'll Need:
Matchboxes (one per participant/team)

Instructions:
1. Give each participant a matchbox and explain they'll be hunting for items small enough to fit inside without damage.
2. Set rules: all items must fit inside the matchbox, no harm should come to nature, and you may set a time limit.
3. Start the hunt, letting participants explore and find small treasures.
4. Once done, gather and check their findings.
5. Reflect on the items found, discussing their significance and encouraging participants to share their favourite discoveries.

This activity is a great way to connect with nature and uncover the small wonders around us!

MARBLES

Materials Needed:
10-15 marbles per player
One larger "bull" marble
A flat playing surface with a small circle marked as the target

Setup:
1. Place the bull marble in the centre of the circle.
2. Players place their marbles equidistant outside the circle.

Gameplay:
1. Players take turns flicking their marbles towards the bull, aiming to knock it out of the circle.
2. If a player knocks the bull out, they win. If they knock other marbles out, they keep them, but the game continues until the bull is knocked out.
3. The game ends when the bull is knocked out, and the player who does so wins.

Rules:
- Flick marbles from outside the circle.
- Keep knuckles on the ground while flicking.

This version requires precision and strategy as players aim to knock the bull out while avoiding obstacles. Enjoy!

SKIPPING

1. Basic Jump Rope: This is the simplest form of skipping, where one or more players jump over the rope as it is swung over their heads and under their feet. Players can try different techniques like single jumps, double jumps, or criss-crossing the rope.

2. Double Dutch: In Double Dutch, two ropes are swung in opposite directions while one or more players jump in and out of the ropes. It requires coordination and timing to avoid getting tangled.

3. Jump Rope Rhymes: These skipping games involve reciting rhymes or chants while jumping rope. Players often use specific rhymes with predetermined patterns to jump to, adding a fun and rhythmic element to the game.

4. Long Rope Jumps: In this game, a long rope is stretched out, and multiple players take turns jumping in and out of the rope while it is being turned by two other players.

5. Criss-Cross: Players jump while the rope is crossed under their feet in an "X" shape. This adds an extra challenge as players must time their jumps to avoid tripping on the crossing rope.

6. Jump the River: Players jump over the rope as it swings low to the ground, imitating the action of jumping over a river. This game can be played individually or in teams.

7. Snake Jump: In this game, one or more players jump over the rope while it is being rotated in a zigzag pattern on the ground, resembling the movement of a snake.

8. Partner Jumps: Two players hold the ends of the rope and swing it while one player jumps. The jumping player can perform various moves like high jumps, twists, or spins while their partner controls the rope.

9. Jump Rope Rhymes: Remember, jump rope rhymes often have variations and can be adapted to fit different rhythms and patterns. These rhymes add a fun and rhythmic element to skipping and help players keep a steady pace while jumping rope. Enjoy!

Teddy Bear, Teddy Bear:
Teddy bear, teddy bear, turn around,
Teddy bear, teddy bear, touch the ground,
Teddy bear, teddy bear, tie your shoe,
Teddy bear, teddy bear, that will do!

Cinderella Dressed in Yellow:
Cinderella dressed in yellow,
Went upstairs to kiss a fellow,

Made a mistake, kissed a snake,
How many doctors did it take?
One, two, three, four…

Bluebells, Cockleshells:
Bluebells, cockleshells,
Evie, ivy, over,
Freezes, sneezes,
Ice cream, soda pop,
We are the girls (boys) from the candy shop.

Apples, Peaches, Pears, and Plums:
Apples, peaches, pears, and plums,
Tell me when your birthday comes,
January, February, March…

Eenie, Meenie, Miney, Mo:
Eenie, meenie, miney, mo,
Catch a tiger by the toe,
If he hollers, let him go,
Out goes you!

HOPSCOTCH

Materials Needed:

Chalk (for the grid)

A small object like a stone or beanbag (the "marker")

Setup:

1. Find a flat surface and clear debris.
2. Draw a hopscotch grid with numbered squares using chalk.

Gameplay:

1. Toss the marker onto the first square.
2. Hop through the grid, skipping the square with the marker, using one foot for single squares and both feet for pairs.
3. Turn around at the end, hop back, and retrieve the marker.
4. If successful, toss the marker onto the next square and repeat.
5. If you make a mistake, your turn ends.
6. The first player to complete the grid wins.

Hopscotch is an easy, fun game that can be played on any flat surface with chalk.

POETRY

Mesostic Poem
A mesostic is a poem or other text arranged so that a vertical phrase intersects lines of horizontal text. It is similar to an acrostic, but with the vertical phrase intersecting somewhere in the midst of the line, as opposed to the beginning of each line.

All
aLone
besiDe
thE
River
by Alec Finlay

Senses Poem
This can easily be adapted to focus on whatever your literacy focus is, from similes to adjectives and more. For different ages/ abilities you can look at drawing the line or creating a paragraph based upon it.

I see...
I hear...
I smell...
I feel...
I think...

Acrostic Poem

An acrostic poem is a poem in which certain letters of each line spell out a word, name, or phrase when read vertically. With younger children I would use simple words for each line, but older children the letter can be the start of a line

Towering majestically
Reaching for the Sky
Earthlings protectors
Eating up our dirty air
So we can all survive

Haiku Poem

This is a traditional Japanese poem focused on nature. Haiku is composed of only 3 lines. There are no more than 17 syllables. Typically, every first line of Haiku has 5 syllables, the second line has 7 syllables, and the third has 5 syllables.

"The Old Pond"
An old silent pond
A frog jumps into the pond –
Splash! Silence again.
by Matsuo Bashō

Fibonacci Poem

This poem also focuses on syllables, but instead follows the Fibonacci sequence
- 1, 1, 2, 3, 5, 8, 13
The first line has one syllable, the second has one, the third two and so on.

1. In
2. gardens
3. growing tall
5. broad beans, green and fat
8. tasting delicious, tummy, sweet

NOTES

Hello,
April

04   APRIL

As April unfolds, everywhere you look, life is bursting forth, with mornings brightening and evenings extending. The gentle breeze carries the scent of fresh growth and new beginnings.

In April, woodlands are often carpeted with bluebells, their delicate, nodding flowers creating a sea of purple-blue. These beautiful blooms thrive in shady areas and are a true sign that spring is in full swing. Bluebells attract early pollinators like bees, which helps spread their reach. Their sweet fragrance fills the air, adding a magical quality to woodland walks. In folklore, bluebells were thought to be enchanted, and it was believed that fairies used them to trap people who wandered too close.

April also brings the "gowk storm," a brief period of cold, wet weather named after the cuckoo. This final reminder of winter adds to the freshness of spring. The rain nurtures the land, making flowers bloom even more vividly.

Despite the unpredictable weather, April is an ideal time to enjoy the outdoors. The changing skies and occasional showers enhance every walk through forests or meadows, where you can see wildflowers and hear birds' lively songs.

04 THE MONTH

Stress Awareness Month
2nd   International Children's Book Day
17th   Haiku Day
18th   World Heritage Day
22nd   World Earth Day
23rd   Shakespeare Day
                St George's Day

Could Do This Month...

♡ _____
♡ _____
♡ _____
♡ _____
♡ _____
♡ _____
♡ _____

04 GARDENING

With April's arrival, it's time to say goodbye to winter vegetables and focus on weeding. Kids often enjoy this task, though it can take a bit of guidance to help them differentiate between weeds and the plants you're growing. To manage this, I always sow extra seeds—typically multiplying by four. This ensures that one quarter will be eaten, another quarter might wilt, a quarter will be enjoyed by bugs and birds, and the last will account for any mistakes made by little hands.

In the greenhouse, I'll get busy sowing more squash and courgettes. Outdoors, it's the perfect time to plant leeks, carrots, beetroot, parsnip, radish, salsify, swede, turnip, onion, and peas. This variety will help ensure a diverse harvest throughout the growing season.

Additionally, I'll start planting potatoes and transferring some of the veggies from my polytunnel or greenhouse, such as cauliflower, beetroot, peas, lettuce, broad beans, onion, and spinach. I find planting in neat, straight lines helps keep things organised and makes weeding much simpler.

04   NIGHT SKY

Full Moon – April 12, 2025
This Full Moon, known as the Pink Moon, will light up the night sky. It's an ideal time for moonlit stargazing, offering a beautiful view as the moon casts its gentle glow.

Lyrid Meteor Shower – Peaking April 22, 2025
The Lyrid meteor shower peaks on the 22nd, with up to 20 meteors per hour. Expect bright, fast streaks across the sky and the occasional fireball. For the best view, look up after midnight in dark skies.

Conjunction of the Moon, Venus, and Saturn – April 26, 2025
Early risers will be treated to a spectacular sight as the Moon, Venus, and Saturn align closely in the pre-dawn sky. This celestial conjunction promises a stunning display just before the sun rises.

The Moon Phases

First Quarter	5TH April
Full Moon	13th April
Last Quarter	21st April
New Moon	27th April

04   WILDLIFE

In ponds and streams, the frogspawn that appeared in March has now hatched into tadpoles, their tiny bodies wriggling in the shallow waters. With each passing day, these small creatures grow, a reminder of the cycle of life that continues all around us.

Capercaillies are a rare and elusive bird. They begin their breeding season in April. Found in the ancient pine forests of places like the Cairngorms, the male capercaillie performs its impressive courtship display, or "lek."

Bottlenose dolphins become more active and visible in coastal areas like the Moray Firth in April. You can spot them from shore or on boat tours as they leap and hunt for fish.

Amphibians like common toads and frogs begin to emerge from their winter dormancy in April, you can spot them in ponds and wetlands across Scotland for breeding.

04   GARDEN LIFE

Birdsong fills the air, as the dawn chorus reaches its peak. Blackbirds, robins, and chaffinches are among the many voices that greet the sunrise, while swallows, newly returned from their winter migration, dart through the sky in graceful arcs, bringing a sense of movement and joy. In the quieter corners of the woods, you might spot woodpeckers nesting, their rhythmic drumming echoing through the trees as they make their homes.

By now, the daffodils that stood proudly through March are joined by a wealth of wildflowers. Bluebells begin to carpet woodland floors in vibrant hues of purple and blue, while the delicate wood anemone dots the ground with its starry white blossoms. The gorse, in full bloom, lines hillsides with bright yellow flowers, their coconut scent carried on the air. These bursts of colour create a stunning contrast against the still-bare trees, which are now slowly cloaked in green as new leaves unfurl.

You may see more bumblebees and butterflies, such as peacocks and small tortoiseshells, visiting flowers like dandelions and forget-me-nots for nectar. Frogs and toads will be active around ponds, with tadpoles hatching and starting to swim.

04   FORAGING

Dandelion

To identify dandelions (Taraxacum officinale) for foraging, look for their bright yellow flowers made up of many small petals. These flowers bloom on long, hollow stems that release a milky sap when broken. The leaves are deeply toothed, lance-shaped, and grow in a rosette pattern at the base of the plant.

Dandelions are commonly found in lawns, fields, and along roadsides. In early spring, they are one of the first flowers to bloom. Every part of the dandelion is edible, from the leaves to the roots. The young leaves are best for salads, while the flowers can be used to make dandelion tea, syrup, or wine. The roots can be roasted and brewed as a coffee substitute.

When foraging, make sure to pick from areas free of pesticides or pollution, and gather only what you need. Dandelions are not only nutritious but also versatile, making them a great addition to various recipes.

04 COOKING

Dandelion Cupcakes

Ingredients:

1 cup dandelion petals (yellow parts only)

1 1/2 cups all-purpose flour

1/2 cup sugar

1/2 cup milk

1/2 cup softened butter

2 eggs

1 tsp vanilla extract

1 1/2 tsp baking powder

A pinch of salt

Instructions:
1. Collect 1 cup of pesticide-free dandelion petals and set aside.
2. Preheat the oven to 180°C (350°F) and line a cupcake tray.
3. In one bowl, mix flour, baking powder, and salt.
4. In another bowl, cream butter and sugar until fluffy, then beat in eggs and vanilla.
5. Fold in dandelion petals and gradually add the flour mixture, alternating with milk.
7. Spoon the batter into liners, filling two-thirds full.
8. Bake for 15-18 minutes, or until a toothpick comes out clean.
9. Cool, then transfer to a wire rack. Frost if desired.

04 THE SEA

Date	\multicolumn{4}{c}{High Water}	\multicolumn{4}{c}{Low Water}
	\multicolumn{2}{c}{Morning}	\multicolumn{2}{c}{Afternoon}	\multicolumn{2}{c}{Morning}	\multicolumn{2}{c}{Afternoon}
	Time	m	Time	m	Time	m	Time	m
1 TU	03 46	5.0	16 00	5.2	09 27	0.7	21 56	0.7
2 W	04 27	4.8	16 47	4.9	10 11	0.9	22 40	1.1
3 TH	05 12	4.5	17 43	4.5	11 01	1.1	23 31	1.6
4 F	06 06	4.2	18 52	4.1			12 02	1.4
5 SA ☽	07 15	3.9	20 15	3.8	00 35	2.0	13 22	1.7
6 **SU**	08 37	3.7	21 53	3.7	02 02	2.3	15 04	1.7
7 M	10 09	3.8	23 17	3.9	03 50	2.3	16 31	1.6
8 TU	11 22	4.0			04 58	2.1	17 26	1.4
9 W	00 12	4.1	12 14	4.2	05 44	1.8	18 09	1.2
10 TH	00 51	4.2	12 52	4.4	06 21	1.6	18 45	1.1
11 F	01 23	4.3	13 26	4.5	06 54	1.4	19 16	1.0
12 SA	01 51	4.4	13 57	4.6	07 25	1.2	19 46	0.9
13 **SU** ○	02 18	4.5	14 27	4.7	07 54	1.2	20 14	1.0
14 M	02 45	4.5	14 57	4.6	08 23	1.1	20 43	1.0
15 TU	03 12	4.5	15 28	4.5	08 52	1.2	21 10	1.2
16 W	03 41	4.5	16 01	4.4	09 21	1.2	21 39	1.4
17 TH	04 11	4.3	16 36	4.2	09 52	1.4	22 11	1.6
18 F	04 44	4.2	17 17	4.0	10 29	1.5	22 47	1.8
19 SA	05 24	4.0	18 08	3.8	11 14	1.7	23 36	2.0
20 **SU**	06 14	3.8	19 18	3.6			12 15	1.9
21 M ☾	07 27	3.6	20 37	3.6	00 48	2.3	13 39	1.9
22 TU	08 48	3.6	21 58	3.7	02 25	2.3	15 09	1.8
23 W	10 03	3.8	23 07	4.0	03 49	2.1	16 21	1.5
24 TH	11 07	4.1	23 59	4.3	04 49	1.8	17 14	1.1
25 F	11 59	4.5			05 35	1.5	18 00	0.8
26 SA	00 43	4.6	12 45	4.8	06 19	1.1	18 43	0.6
27 **SU** ●	01 23	4.8	13 28	5.1	07 00	0.9	19 26	0.4
28 M	02 02	5.0	14 12	5.2	07 42	0.7	20 09	0.5
29 TU	02 42	5.0	14 59	5.2	08 26	0.6	20 52	0.7
30 W	03 23	4.9	15 47	5.0	09 12	0.7	21 36	1.0

HEIGHTS ABOVE CHART DATUM

Time Zone UT(GMT)

04 SCAVENGER

Bird Song

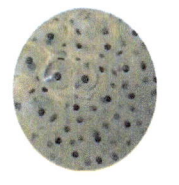

Frog Spawn

Hazel Catkins

Birds Nesting

Bluebells

Worms

Tree Buds

Blossom

Seedling

Daffodil

Bees

Snowdrops

GREEN MAN

There have been stories of green men told for centuries and across many countries. Whilst he can mean different things to different people, he often represents an environmental guardian and keeper of the forest. As teachers, we have a responsibility to teach sustainability. The green man can be a useful cross-curricular tool in exploring this.

We often tell a story when working with children in nursery all the way up to secondary; unfortunately, I do not know the origin of it nor the true version, yet children enjoy it, and it sparks their imagination. The story goes...

Once upon a time, there lived a rich and vain young prince. Servants prepared his favourite foods each day. His every wish was granted. He cared not for people nor animals.

One hot day, the young prince decided to ride his horse through the woods that were part of his kingdom, hunting small animals for fun. He thought that the woods and all its creatures belonged to him, and he could do as he pleased with them. He raced over the woods and fields, scaring many creatures as he went.

It was a hot day, and he needed to cool down. He came to a loch — a beautiful, clear, cool loch.

The young man began to remove all of his fine clothing. He laid his clothes neatly folded on an old log and by the edge of the loch and tied his horse to a tree before jumping into the cool water.

While he was swimming and splashing away, a hand reached out from behind a tree and took his clothing and led his horse away. When the prince got out of the water, he discovered that he had nothing left to wear save a piece of rope. He took the rope and fastened some leaves to it to make a cover up. He was a proud and vain prince. He could not go back to his home dressed like this, so instead he hid.

At night, the prince went looking for some shelter and he stumbled into a cave. He didn't sleep much that night. It was dark, and he was frightened, and he kept hearing animal noises all night.

In the morning, when the daylight came, it was clear that someone had been living in that cave! He found some food, bedding and a container for water.

Over time, the prince settled into life in the cave. He fashioned a whole garment out of leaves. He ate from the land. He covered his hand with mud to prevent stings and reached into a beehive for honey to eat. He became acquainted with all the small woodland creatures, and he cared for them, helping them over swollen streams when heavy rains fell, making sure they had food and water, and sheltering them in the cave on the chilly nights.

One day, whilst out walking he heard the screams of some scared children. Raced towards the screams and discovered two small children trapped by a wild pig threatening to charge. When he had chased the pig off, they looked at him. There he was, covered head to toe with leaves and mud, with a wild-looking beard and hair.

"Are you the Green Man?" they asked.

"I guess I am," said the man, who no longer looked anything like a prince.

The children went back to the village and told their adults of the Green Man. As time passed, the villagers told their children a story about a Green Man who lived in the woods and cared for all of the small creatures. They said he even watched out for children in the woods. The villagers faithfully left out food on winter nights for the Green Man to eat.

Many years passed, until one warm day when a hunting party came into the woods. The Green Man hid behind a tree to watch. A rich young man, a prince perhaps, became separated from his hunting group and decided to take a swim in the clear, cool loch. He took off his clothes, folded them, and left them under a tree.

The Green Man reached out a hand and took the clothes and the horse, leaving behind his garment of leaves and a coil of rope. He used a sharp stick to trim his hair and beard, and rode into town, back to his parents' castle.

Some questions you could ask the children are:
Who would be the green man now?
What does he need to protect?
Who looks after the forests now?
Why do they need to be looked after?
Why might so many cultures across the world have green man myths?

Some activities you could try are:
Create green men using clay or found materials
Create homes for animals
Build a den for the green man

LOCAL HISTORY EXPLORATION

Objective:
Help children explore and appreciate local history by investigating landmarks, buildings, and community evolution through outdoor exploration.

What You'll Need:
Paper and pens
Cameras or tablets (optional)
Clipboards (optional)

Instructions:
1. Discuss local history with the children, asking what they know about the area's evolution.
2. Lead an indoor discussion on how buildings, transportation, and the community have changed.
3. Take the children outside to explore the area, acting as reporters searching for historical clues. They should note or photograph key items like bus stops, old buildings, and landmarks.
4. Back inside, have children share and discuss their findings, reflecting on how these clues explain the area's development.
5. Ask reflection questions like what surprised them, how the area has changed, and what clues helped them understand the local history.

6. Summarise key learnings and encourage continued exploration of local history.

Why It's Great:
- Encourages hands-on learning and deeper connections with the community.
- Develops critical thinking, note-taking, and observational skills.

Remember:
This activity merges history with outdoor learning, helping children appreciate their area's changes over time.

NOTES

Hello, May

05 MAY

As May arrives, spring is in full bloom across Scotland. The days are long and bright, the air warm, and the landscape bursts with vibrant life. Everything feels alive with the energy of renewal, inviting us to step outside and enjoy the full splendour of spring.

The hawthorn, or "May Tree," is a highlight of this month, adorned with white or pink blossoms that fill the air with a delicate fragrance. In Scottish folklore, the hawthorn is linked to Beltane, an ancient festival celebrating summer's arrival. It's believed that faeries were especially active around hawthorn trees in May, making them symbols of protection and abundance for those who respected them.

Despite the warmth, folklore advises caution. The old saying "Ne'er cast a clout till May be oot" reminds us that late frosts are still possible until the hawthorn blooms. Washing your face in May dew was said to bring beauty and good fortune, but planting crops too early could lead to trouble.

May is a perfect time to immerse yourself in nature. Whether walking through meadows, enjoying birdsong, or relaxing by a river, the outdoors in May is full of life and optimism.

05 THE MONTH

Mental Health Awareness Month

4th	Dawn Chorus Day
5th	National Hedgerow Week
	Compost Week
9th	Europe Day
11th	Children's Day
12th	Sun Awareness Week
14th	Be Nice to Nettles Day
19th	Walk to School Week
20th	World Bee Day
22nd	Outdoor Classroom Day
	Biological Diversity Day
23rd	Turtle Day

Could Do This Month...

♡ _____
♡ _____
♡ _____
♡ _____
♡ _____
♡ _____
♡ _____

05 GARDENING

In gardens and hedgerows, elderflowers begin to bloom, their creamy white clusters spreading across the landscape, soon to be harvested for refreshing cordials and wines. The air in May is sweet, filled with the scent of blossoms and the freshness of new growth.

In May I love looking at my garden, as it looks like a wonderful productive space (even if the deer are eating everything within sight!). I stake my peas and beans, which is just a fancy way of saying I pop some bamboo into the ground with string to help them grow. I am now well into the weeding season.

In my greenhouse/ polytunnel I am sowing sprouts, runner beans and French beans and broccoli
And you will find me planting out my tomatoes, courgette, squash

The hard work should be starting to pay off as I can harvest salad, radish, spinach, salad onion – a lovely springtime salad!

05   NIGHT SKY

Eta Aquariid Meteor Shower – May 6, 2025
This annual meteor shower, originating from debris left by Halley's Comet, will peak in early May. The best viewing times will be in the early morning hours, with up to 30 meteors per hour under dark skies, however, it is close to the full moon so may be hard to spot.

Full Moon – May 12, 2025
The Full Moon will brighten the night sky. It's sometimes referred to as the Flower Moon, signalling the bloom of spring flowers.

Venus at Greatest Elongation West – May 31, 2025
Venus will reach its greatest distance from the Sun in the morning sky. This will be a perfect time to observe Venus shining brightly in the early hours before sunrise.

The Moon Phases

First Quarter	4TH May
Full Moon	12th May
Last Quarter	20th May
New Moon	27th May

05 WILDLIFE

May is a vibrant time for birdlife, with the dawn chorus in full swing as blackbirds, wrens, and warblers sing, and swallows and house martins swoop above. In quieter woods, fledglings take their first steps into the world.

Rivers and streams are alive with young fish and dragonflies darting above the water. The rivers reflect the lush greenery surrounding them, adding to the sense of seasonal vitality.

Woodlands are stunning, with bluebells carpeting the forest floor and the canopy lush with new growth. Ferns unfurl gracefully, enhancing the rich undergrowth.

May also marks the start of basking shark season along Scotland's west coast, especially around the Hebrides, where these gentle giants feed on plankton. Pine martens become more active, hunting in Scotland's woodlands, and Great Crested Grebes perform their striking courtship dances on lochs and lakes.

05   GARDEN LIFE

The fields and meadows are alive with wildflowers. Buttercups, daisies, and red campion brighten the green fields, while the first orchids start to appear, adding a touch of the exotic to the Scottish countryside. Bumblebees buzz from flower to flower, their wings a constant hum as they gather nectar, while butterflies like the orange-tip flit gracefully among the blossoms.

In May, your garden in Scotland will be bustling with life as spring reaches its peak. Birds will be feeding their young, with parents frequently visiting feeders to gather food for their chicks. You'll notice more pollinators, such as bees and butterflies, as they take advantage of the blooming flowers like bluebells, tulips, and hawthorn. Hedgehogs, fully active after hibernation, may be seen foraging in the evenings, especially if your garden offers food and shelter. Ponds will also be lively, with tadpoles developing into froglets. May is an exciting time for garden wildlife as the warmer weather encourages even more activity.

05   FORAGING

Nettle

To identify nettles (Urtica dioica) for foraging, look for their jagged, heart-shaped leaves with serrated edges. The leaves grow opposite each other on long, fibrous stems that are covered in tiny, stinging hairs. These hairs can cause a mild skin irritation if touched, which is why gloves are recommended when harvesting. Nettles can grow quite tall, often reaching up to 1.5 metres in height.

Nettles are typically found in nutrient-rich soil along riverbanks, in woodlands, or near fields. They are best harvested in early spring when the young leaves are tender. As the plant matures, the leaves become tougher and less palatable.

When foraging, pick only the top few leaves, as these are the most tender and nutritious. Once cooked or dried, the stinging hairs lose their potency, making nettles safe to eat. Nettles are packed with nutrients and can be used in soup, tea, pesto, and as a spinach substitute in various dishes. Always ensure you're foraging in a pesticide-free area, and harvest sustainably by leaving plenty of plants behind to continue growing.

05 COOKING

Nettle Soup

A classic way to enjoy nettles, similar to spinach soup but with a foraged twist.

Ingredients:

1 onion, chopped
1 garlic clove, minced
1 potato, peeled and chopped
A large handful of fresh nettle leaves (only use the young, tender ones)
500ml vegetable stock
1 tbsp olive oil
Salt and pepper to taste

Instructions:

1. Heat olive oil in a pot and sauté the onion and garlic until soft.
2. Add the potato and vegetable stock, and simmer until the potato is tender (about 10-15 minutes).
3. Add the nettle leaves and cook for another 2-3 minutes until wilted.
4. Blend the soup until smooth, then season with salt and pepper. Serve with a drizzle of cream or olive oil.

05 THE SEA

Date	HEIGHTS ABOVE CHART DATUM						
	High Water				Low Water			
	Morning		Afternoon		Morning		Afternoon	
	Time	m	Time	m	Time	m	Time	m
1 TH	04 07	4.7	16 40	4.7	10 02	0.8	22 24	1.3
2 F	04 55	4.5	17 40	4.4	10 55	1.0	23 17	1.7
3 SA	05 50	4.2	18 47	4.1	11 59	1.3		
4 SU ☽	06 57	4.0	20 00	3.8	00 20	2.1	13 13	1.5
5 M	08 11	3.9	21 21	3.7	01 39	2.3	14 35	1.6
6 TU	09 30	3.8	22 37	3.8	03 05	2.3	15 53	1.5
7 W	10 41	3.9	23 32	3.9	04 16	2.1	16 49	1.4
8 TH	11 35	4.1			05 07	1.9	17 32	1.3
9 F	00 13	4.1	12 18	4.2	05 47	1.7	18 09	1.3
10 SA	00 48	4.2	12 55	4.3	06 22	1.5	18 41	1.2
11 SU	01 18	4.3	13 29	4.4	06 56	1.4	19 13	1.2
12 M ○	01 48	4.4	14 02	4.5	07 29	1.3	19 44	1.2
13 TU	02 17	4.5	14 36	4.4	08 00	1.2	20 14	1.2
14 W	02 47	4.5	15 10	4.4	08 32	1.2	20 46	1.3
15 TH	03 17	4.5	15 45	4.3	09 06	1.3	21 18	1.5
16 F	03 50	4.4	16 23	4.2	09 41	1.3	21 54	1.6
17 SA	04 25	4.3	17 07	4.0	10 22	1.4	22 35	1.8
18 SU	05 07	4.1	17 58	3.9	11 10	1.5	23 26	1.9
19 M	05 56	4.0	19 01	3.8			12 07	1.6
20 TU ☾	07 00	3.9	20 08	3.8	00 31	2.1	13 17	1.6
21 W	08 11	3.9	21 17	3.9	01 47	2.1	14 29	1.5
22 TH	09 19	4.0	22 22	4.1	03 00	2.0	15 35	1.3
23 F	10 24	4.2	23 20	4.3	04 03	1.8	16 34	1.1
24 SA	11 23	4.5			04 59	1.5	17 26	0.9
25 SU	00 10	4.5	12 18	4.8	05 49	1.2	18 16	0.8
26 M	00 55	4.7	13 08	4.9	06 37	1.0	19 03	0.8
27 TU ●	01 39	4.8	13 59	5.0	07 25	0.8	19 50	0.8
28 W	02 22	4.9	14 49	5.0	08 14	0.7	20 36	1.0
29 TH	03 07	4.9	15 41	4.8	09 05	0.7	21 24	1.2
30 F	03 53	4.8	16 35	4.6	09 56	0.8	22 12	1.5
31 SA	04 42	4.6	17 33	4.4	10 49	0.9	23 02	1.7

Time Zone UT(GMT)

05   SCAVENGER

Did you know...
There are over 25,000 minibeast species in the UK alone!

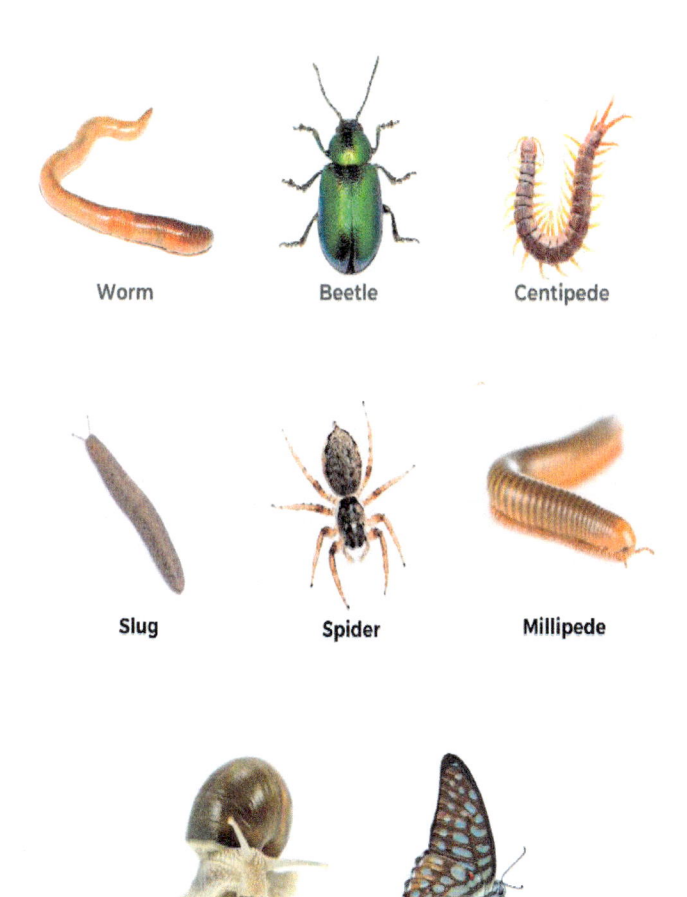

| Worm | Beetle | Centipede |

| Slug | Spider | Millipede |

| Snail | Butterfly |

MINI COMPOST

Materials:
Plastic bottle (label removed)
Black paint
Sharp knife (adult supervision needed)
Duct tape
Shredded paper or dry leaves
Vegetable scraps, coffee grounds, eggshells
Spray bottle (optional)

Instructions:
1. Remove the label and paint the bottle black to absorb heat.
2. With adult supervision, cut a door (5x3 inches) in the side of the bottle, leaving one side as a hinge.
3. Punch air holes every 10-15 cm around the bottle.
4. Layer shredded paper/leaves at the bottom, then add vegetable scraps, coffee grounds, or eggshells. Moisten slightly.
5. Close the door with duct tape and place the bottle in sunlight.
6. Check moisture daily and mix by rolling the bottle. Add paper if too wet or mist if too dry. Compost is ready in about 30 days.

The Science:

1. Decomposition: Microorganisms break down organic matter, releasing nutrients like nitrogen and phosphorus.
2. Aeration: Air holes promote aerobic decomposition, preventing bad smells and speeding up the process.
3. Heat: The black bottle absorbs heat, speeding up microbial activity and decomposition.
4. Moisture: Proper moisture is crucial for microbes. Too much water slows the process, so balancing is key.

This mini compost bin demonstrates how organic waste breaks down into nutrient-rich compost for sustainable gardening.

BIO BLITZ

Objective:
Conduct a BioBlitz to help children observe and record local biodiversity, fostering their connection with nature.

What You'll Need:
Timer
Area map (optional)
Quadrats/hoops for marking areas
Paper and pens for recording
Cameras/tablets for photos (optional)
RSPB guides or ID books

Instructions:
1. Set the time: Decide how long the survey will last (e.g., 15 minutes).
2. Survey area: Mark out spots for each group to explore using a map (optional).
3. Observe and count: Place quadrats/hoops in each area and count all living things in that spot.
4. Identify: Use guides or take photos to identify plants and animals.
5. Record findings: Document observations and compare results across locations.

Survey 2:

Repeat the survey after a few weeks in the same locations, comparing results to observe seasonal changes.

Why It's Great:
- Sparks curiosity about biodiversity.
- Encourages outdoor exploration.
- Develops observation and recording skills.

Remember:
Conducting the BioBlitz at different times of year helps children see how seasons affect biodiversity and fosters a lasting interest in nature.

NOTES

Hello,
June

06 JUNE

June arrives in full bloom, and Scotland feels alive with the transition from spring into early summer. The days are long, with the sun lingering in the sky until late in the evening, casting a golden light over the landscape.

June is also the month of midsummer, celebrated in Scottish folklore as a time of magic and light. The summer solstice, when the day is longest, was traditionally marked with bonfires and festivals, as people celebrated the abundance of the season and the power of the sun. Some believed that this was when the boundary between our world and the faerie world was thin, so wandering the woods on midsummer's eve held the promise of magic.

June offers endless opportunities to explore the outdoors, whether it's wandering through flower-filled meadows, taking a peaceful walk in the cool shade of the woods, or heading to the coast to spot seabirds and marine life. The days are long, the nights are short, and nature is at its most abundant. Take advantage of the warm weather and immerse yourself in the beauty that surrounds you—it's a time to enjoy the bounty of the season and feel rejuvenated by the energy of the natural world.

06   THE MONTH

1st	Dinosaur Day
2nd	Child Safety Week
3rd	World Bicycle Day
3rd	Farming Fortnight
5th	World Environment Day
7th	Big Green Week
8th	World Oceans Day
11th	International Day of Play
13th	School Grounds Week
15th	Global Wind Day
16th	Den Day
16th	Children's Art Week
21st	Summer Solstice
	Make Music Day
22nd	World Rainforest Day
23rd	World Insect Week
26th	Garden Wildlife Week
29th	International Mud Week

Could Do This Month...

♡ _____
♡ _____
♡ _____
♡ _____

06 GARDENING

In the gardens and fields, the early harvests begin. Strawberries ripen under the June sun, their sweet, red fruit a highlight of the season. Many families take the opportunity to pick fresh berries from local farms, bringing a taste of summer home with them. Rhubarb, too, is plentiful, its sharp flavour pairing perfectly with the season's sweetness. The vegetable gardens are lush with growth, with peas, broad beans, and early potatoes ready to be picked, and the first signs of summer crops beginning to appear.

It is June and the summer holidays are close. I have hopefully taken the time to build community links to help support and learn from. If you are in a school, they may even be able to water the plants during the holidays.

I can sow broccoli, swede, lettuce, carrots, and beetroot outside now. I can also plant on the sprouts, beans, cucumber, tomato that I have started indoors and, at the end month my swede, leek.

Harvest wise, I can be collecting my beetroot, carrots, spuds, courgette, cauliflower, lettuce, broad beans, peas – such a lot!

06   NIGHT SKY

The persistent twilight of summer can make it hard to spot much this month, especially for those who are further north.

Full Moon – June 11, 2025
The Full Moon will illuminate the sky, often referred to as the Strawberry Moon. This bright lunar event will dominate the night sky, making it a great time for moonlit activities.

Daytime Arietid Meteor Shower – June 10, 2025
This meteor shower is one of the strongest daytime showers, peaking around this time. Though the best viewing happens before dawn, some meteors may be visible during twilight.

June Solstice – June 21, 2025
Marking the start of summer, the longest day of the year will occur on June 21. The summer solstice is a major celestial event when the Sun reaches its highest point in the sky.

The Moon Phases

First Quarter	3rd June
Full Moon	11th June
Last Quarter	18th June
New Moon	25th June

06 WILDLIFE

In June, the woodlands come alive with the soft rustling of leaves as the dense canopy offers a cool, shady retreat from the height of summer. The fully unfurled leaves dance gently in the warm breeze, creating a peaceful backdrop for long woodland walks. Ferns, now at their tallest, add to the lush green undergrowth, making the forest floor a place of thriving life.

In the countryside, the pastures are rich and vibrant, butterflies, such as the painted lady, small tortoiseshell, and peacock, flit from flower to flower, bringing bursts of colour and life to the already lively landscape.

June is also prime time for spotting golden eagles soaring high over Scotland's Highlands and Islands. These magnificent birds of prey can often be seen hunting in the remote mountain regions, particularly in places like the Cairngorms and Skye.

As the long daylight hours fade into dusk, badgers become active, foraging near their setts in the woodlands. Rural areas like the Borders and Dumfries and Galloway offer a better chance of spotting these elusive creatures as they venture out in the cool evening air.

06   GARDEN LIFE

The fields and meadows are alive with wildflowers. Buttercups, daisies, and red campion brighten the green fields, while the first orchids start to appear, adding a touch of the exotic to the Scottish countryside. Bumblebees buzz from flower to flower, their wings a constant hum as they gather nectar, while butterflies like the orange-tip flit gracefully among the blossoms.

In June, your garden in Scotland will be thriving with summer wildlife activity. Birds such as sparrows, finches, and starlings will be busy feeding their fledglings, and you'll likely see young birds learning to fly and forage. Bees, butterflies, and other pollinators will be abundant, attracted to the blooming flowers like lavender, foxgloves, and wildflowers, providing essential nectar sources. Hedgehogs are particularly active at dusk, foraging for insects and slugs. If you have a pond, dragonflies and damselflies may be spotted hovering near the water, and frogs or newts might be more visible as they explore. June is a vibrant month for garden wildlife, with many species at their busiest.

06   FORAGING

Elderflower

To identify elderflower (Sambucus nigra) for foraging, look for its creamy-white flower clusters that bloom in late spring to early summer. The flowers grow in flat-topped, umbrella-shaped clusters known as umbels and have a sweet, fragrant smell. Each cluster is made up of tiny, five-petaled flowers.

The elderflower tree or shrub is easily recognizable by its light grey-brown bark and pinnate leaves, which have 5-7 serrated leaflets. Elder trees often grow in hedgerows, woodlands, and along roadsides.
When foraging, pick the flower heads on a dry, sunny day when they are fully open, as they will be the most fragrant at this time. Avoid harvesting from areas near roadsides or polluted areas. The flowers should be used quickly after picking, as they wilt fast, or they can be dried for later use.

Elderflowers are versatile and can be used to make cordials, syrups, teas, or even infused into honey or vinegar. Always ensure you are foraging from the correct elder plant and avoid any toxic lookalikes, such as dwarf elder, which has similar flowers but is not safe to consume.

06 COOKING

Elderflower-Infused Honey

An easy way to capture the floral essence of elderflowers and use it throughout the year.

Ingredients:

Fresh elderflower heads (5-6 large heads)
1 jar of honey

Instructions:

1. Remove the elderflower heads from their stems, keeping only the small flowers.
2. Warm the honey slightly to make it easier to mix (but don't overheat it).
3. Stir the elderflowers into the honey.
4. Let the mixture sit for 1-2 weeks, stirring occasionally.
5. Strain the honey to remove the flowers, then store in a jar. Use in teas, on toast, or in desserts.

06 THE SEA

Date		High Water Morning Time	m	High Water Afternoon Time	m	Low Water Morning Time	m	Low Water Afternoon Time	m
1	SU	05 35	4.4	18 29	4.1	11 46	1.1	23 57	1.9
2	M	06 33	4.2	19 27	3.9			12 46	1.3
3	TU ☽	07 33	4.0	20 30	3.7	00 58	2.1	13 48	1.5
4	W	08 37	3.9	21 35	3.7	02 03	2.2	14 50	1.6
5	TH	09 44	3.9	22 36	3.8	03 11	2.2	15 53	1.6
6	F	10 46	3.9	23 25	3.9	04 15	2.0	16 45	1.6
7	SA	11 38	4.0			05 08	1.9	17 28	1.5
8	SU	00 08	4.0	12 24	4.1	05 51	1.7	18 08	1.5
9	M	00 46	4.2	13 05	4.2	06 29	1.6	18 43	1.4
10	TU	01 21	4.3	13 43	4.3	07 07	1.4	19 19	1.4
11	W ○	01 55	4.4	14 20	4.3	07 42	1.3	19 54	1.4
12	TH	02 27	4.5	14 58	4.3	08 18	1.3	20 29	1.4
13	F	03 01	4.5	15 35	4.3	08 56	1.2	21 06	1.5
14	SA	03 35	4.5	16 16	4.3	09 35	1.2	21 45	1.5
15	SU	04 13	4.4	16 58	4.2	10 17	1.2	22 27	1.6
16	M	04 54	4.4	17 45	4.1	11 02	1.2	23 14	1.7
17	TU	05 40	4.3	18 37	4.0	11 53	1.3		
18	W ☾	06 34	4.3	19 35	4.0	00 06	1.8	12 50	1.3
19	TH	07 35	4.2	20 37	4.0	01 08	1.8	13 51	1.3
20	F	08 39	4.2	21 41	4.1	02 14	1.8	14 53	1.3
21	SA	09 47	4.3	22 45	4.2	03 20	1.8	15 57	1.3
22	SU	10 55	4.4	23 44	4.3	04 25	1.6	17 00	1.2
23	M			12 01	4.5	05 28	1.4	17 58	1.2
24	TU	00 36	4.5	12 59	4.7	06 25	1.2	18 51	1.2
25	W ●	01 25	4.7	13 54	4.8	07 19	0.9	19 40	1.2
26	TH	02 11	4.8	14 46	4.8	08 09	0.8	20 27	1.2
27	F	02 57	4.8	15 36	4.7	08 59	0.7	21 13	1.3
28	SA	03 41	4.8	16 24	4.6	09 47	0.7	21 56	1.4
29	SU	04 26	4.7	17 12	4.4	10 34	0.8	22 39	1.6
30	M	05 12	4.6	17 58	4.2	11 21	1.0	23 22	1.7

Time Zone UT(GMT)

06   SCAVENGER

Dandelion

Nettle

Chickweed

Cleavers/
Sticky willie

Garlic Mustard

Hairy
Bittercress

Doc

Disy

Ground
Elder

"A weed is just a flower in the wrong place."
— Cecilia Ahern

SHADOW HUNTERS

Objective:
Encourage creativity and connection with nature by creating silhouette art using sunlight and natural materials.

Materials:
Chalk or water and paintbrushes
Natural materials (leaves, twigs, stones)
Paper (optional)
Access to sunlight

Instructions:
1. Explain the activity and how sunlight and shadows will be used to create art by outlining shadows with chalk or natural materials.
2. Pair children and have one create a shadow while the other outlines it using chalk, water, or natural materials. Encourage experimentation with layering and blending.
3. Each pair presents their artwork, sharing the process and materials they used.
4. Discuss the experience and how sunlight and natural materials influenced their designs.
5. Allow time for tidying up.

Why It's Great:
- Fosters creativity and teamwork using natural elements.
- Encourages outdoor exploration and enhances observational skills.

Remember:
Supervise children and ensure they handle materials safely while engaging with nature creatively.

SISTRUM

Materials Needed:

A sturdy Y shaped twig (about 20 -40 cm long)
Bottle tops (10-15, depending on the length of the twig). Metal beer bottle tops work best
Thin wire or strong thread
Hammer and nail (for making holes in bottle tops)
Sandpaper (optional, for smoothing the twig)

Instructions:

1. Select a sturdy, y shaped twig that is about 30-40 cm long. Remove any leaves or small branches. If desired, use sandpaper to smooth the twig and remove any rough spots.
2. Collect 10-15 bottle tops. The exact number depends on the length of the twig and your preference for how many jingles you want on your sistrum.
3. Use a hammer and nail to make two small holes near the edge of each bottle top, directly opposite each other. Ensure the holes are large enough to thread wire or string through.
4. Cut a piece of thin wire or strong thread. The piece should reach across from one side of the Y to the other and have 10-15cm extra to allow you to attach it securely. Thread each bottle top onto the wire. I

tend to do it in pairs, with the back of 2 facing each other.
5. Twist the ends of the wire together or tie the thread securely to ensure the bottle tops stay in place.
6. Make sure all the bottle tops are securely fastened and can move slightly to create the jingling sound when shaken. Adjust the spacing if needed to ensure an even distribution of sound.
7. You can decorate your sistrum by wrapping colourful thread or ribbons around the twig. Add beads or other small decorative elements to the wire or thread for added visual appeal.

ONLY USE TOOLS IF YOU HAVE BEEN TRAINED AND ARE COMPETENT

BE CAREFUL NOT TO HURT YOURSELF

IF CHILDREN ARE USING TOOLS, THEY SHOULD BE CLOSELY SUPERVISED AT ALL TIMES

NOTES

Hello,
July

07 JULY

July bursts onto the scene with the full embrace of summer, and Scotland is drenched in warmth and light. The long, bright days stretch well into the evening, and the landscape thrives under the sun's steady glow. July is a time to embrace the outdoors, to immerse yourself in the beauty and abundance of summer.

Many birds are raising their young, and if you look closely, you might spot fledglings testing their wings and learning to fly.

Scottish folklore speaks of these summer months as a time of faerie activity, with the long twilight hours believed to be a magical time. There's a quiet beauty in those lingering evenings, perfect for slowing down and appreciating the world around you.

Getting outdoors in July is all about soaking in the warmth, light, and life of summer. Whether you're walking through meadows of wildflowers, exploring the shady trails of a woodland, or heading to the coast to watch seabirds and seals, the natural world is at its most inviting. The long daylight hours give you plenty of time to explore, relax, and reconnect with nature.

07 THE MONTH

Plastic Free July
National Picnic Month

1st	Clean Beaches Week
10th	Don't Step on a Bee Day
17th (to 10 Aug)	Big Butterfly Count
19th	National Moth Week
24th	National Marine Week
25th	Love Park Weeks

Could Do This Month...

- ♡ _____
- ♡ _____
- ♡ _____
- ♡ _____
- ♡ _____
- ♡ _____
- ♡ _____

07 GARDENING

July brings a wealth of fresh produce, and the harvest season is well underway. Berry picking becomes a favourite activity, with raspberries, strawberries, and blackcurrants ripe for the picking. The taste of freshly picked summer berries, warmed by the sun, is one of the great joys of the season.

Gardens are brimming with vegetables—courgettes, peas, and beans grow abundantly, while the first tomatoes begin to ripen on the vine. Whether in your own garden or at local farms, July offers an abundance of fresh, local produce to enjoy.

As I am weeding this month, I am also spreading a thick layer of compost, just to perk my beds up.
My sowing is slowing with just lettuce and winter salad going down.

I can plant my swede, cauli, broccoli and beetroot outdoors.

Harvest is starting to get a little lighter, with spuds, peas, broad beans, and courgettes being collected this month.

07 NIGHT SKY

Planetary Conjunctions - July 19-20, 2025
you'll be able to witness a rare conjunction of Mercury, Venus, and Mars. This trio, along with a crescent Moon, will be visible in the western sky shortly after sunset.

Milky Way Viewing - Throughout Summer
July is also one of the best months to observe the core of the Milky Way in the constellation Sagittarius, visible low in the southern sky. The dense star fields and dark dust lanes make for an impressive sight, especially under clear, dark skies.

The Full Moon in July 2025 - July 12, 2025
This Full Moon is often referred to as the Buck Moon, as it traditionally marks the time when male deer begin to grow their new antlers

The Moon Phases

First Quarter	2nd July
Full Moon	10th July
Last Quarter	18th July
New Moon	24th July

07 WILDLIFE

The wildflower meadows, so full of colour in June, are now a sea of motion, as bees and butterflies flit from flower to flower, busy collecting nectar. Poppies, cornflowers, and knapweed add bold splashes of red, blue, and purple, standing tall against the golden grasses swaying in the warm breeze. The fields are alive with life, from buzzing insects to the calls of skylarks high above.

Woodlands are lush and dense, providing cool, shady retreats from the heat of the day. The air is rich with the scent of pine and earth, and the gentle rustle of leaves creates a calming backdrop to any walk. Ferns have reached their full, impressive height, and the bracken forms a green underlayer beneath towering trees. Exploring forest trails is a wonderful way to experience the peaceful side of summer, with dappled sunlight filtering through the canopy above.

Along Scotland's coastlines, summer reaches its peak in July. Seabird colonies, now bustling with activity, continue their busy lives on cliffs and rocky shores. Puffins, with their bright orange beaks, return from fishing trips to feed their young, while gulls and terns fill the air with their calls. It's the perfect time to explore the coast, take a boat trip, or simply walk along the shoreline and watch the waves.

07   GARDEN LIFE

The fields and meadows are alive with wildflowers. Buttercups, daisies, and red campion brighten the green fields, while the first orchids start to appear, adding a touch of the exotic to the Scottish countryside. Bumblebees buzz from flower to flower, their wings a constant hum as they gather nectar, while butterflies like the orange-tip flit gracefully among the blossoms.

In July, your garden in Scotland will be buzzing with summer wildlife at its peak. Butterflies, such as red admirals and peacocks, are frequent visitors, fluttering around nectar-rich flowers like buddleia and lavender. Bees continue to thrive, gathering pollen from blooming plants. Birds, including sparrows, blackbirds, and finches, will still be seen feeding their young, with fledglings exploring the garden. Hedgehogs remain active in the evenings, searching for food like insects and slugs. If you have a pond, you may spot frogs, toads, or newts basking near the water's edge. July brings a lively mix of wildlife, making the garden a thriving summer ecosystem.

07   FORAGING

Raspberry

To identify raspberries (Rubus idaeus), look for small, red, clustered berries growing on thorny, arching canes. The berries consist of tiny drupelets and have a hollow core when picked. The toothed leaves are divided into three to five leaflets, and the stems have fine, less aggressive thorns compared to blackberries.

Raspberries thrive in sunny spots like woodland edges, clearings, and hedgerows. They grow in dense thickets and prefer well-drained soil. The best time to forage is from July to September when the berries are bright red and easy to pick.

Forage by gently picking ripe berries, avoiding crushed fruit and thorny stems. Stay away from areas near roads or treated with chemicals. Wild raspberries are great fresh or in jams and desserts. Always forage responsibly, leaving plenty for wildlife and future growth.

07 COOKING

Raspberry and Mint Salad
A light and refreshing summer salad, perfect as a side dish or snack.

Ingredients:
1 cup fresh raspberries
A handful of fresh mint leaves, torn
1 cucumber, sliced
A drizzle of olive oil
A squeeze of lemon juice
Salt and pepper to taste

Instructions:
1. Combine the raspberries, mint, and cucumber in a bowl.
2. Drizzle with olive oil and lemon juice.
3. Season with salt and pepper, then gently toss to mix.
4. Serve as a side salad or a light snack.

07 THE SEA

	HEIGHTS ABOVE CHART DATUM							
	High Water				Low Water			
Date	Morning		Afternoon		Morning		Afternoon	
	Time	m	Time	m	Time	m	Time	m
1 TU	05 59	4.4	18 45	4.0			12 06	1.2
2 W ☽	06 48	4.2	19 34	3.8	00 08	1.9	12 55	1.4
3 TH	07 40	4.0	20 28	3.7	01 00	2.0	13 45	1.6
4 F	08 39	3.8	21 27	3.7	02 00	2.1	14 42	1.8
5 SA	09 46	3.8	22 30	3.7	03 07	2.2	15 44	1.9
6 SU	10 55	3.8	23 27	3.9	04 20	2.1	16 46	1.9
7 M	11 55	3.9			05 21	2.0	17 38	1.8
8 TU	00 16	4.0	12 45	4.0	06 09	1.8	18 20	1.7
9 W	00 57	4.2	13 28	4.1	06 49	1.6	19 00	1.6
10 TH ○	01 36	4.4	14 07	4.3	07 27	1.4	19 38	1.5
11 F	02 11	4.5	14 45	4.4	08 05	1.2	20 15	1.4
12 SA	02 46	4.6	15 23	4.5	08 44	1.0	20 54	1.3
13 SU	03 21	4.7	16 02	4.5	09 23	0.9	21 32	1.3
14 M	03 59	4.7	16 41	4.5	10 04	0.9	22 12	1.3
15 TU	04 37	4.7	17 23	4.4	10 45	0.9	22 52	1.4
16 W	05 20	4.7	18 09	4.3	11 30	1.0	23 38	1.5
17 TH	06 07	4.6	19 00	4.2			12 18	1.1
18 F ☾	07 02	4.5	19 59	4.1	00 32	1.7	13 15	1.3
19 SA	08 08	4.3	21 05	4.0	01 35	1.8	14 18	1.5
20 SU	09 22	4.2	22 16	4.0	02 47	1.8	15 29	1.6
21 M	10 43	4.2	23 26	4.2	04 06	1.8	16 47	1.6
22 TU	11 59	4.3			05 23	1.5	17 53	1.6
23 W	00 27	4.4	13 02	4.5	06 23	1.3	18 46	1.5
24 TH ●	01 18	4.6	13 55	4.6	07 17	1.0	19 34	1.4
25 F	02 03	4.8	14 41	4.7	08 04	0.8	20 16	1.3
26 SA	02 45	4.9	15 23	4.7	08 49	0.7	20 56	1.3
27 SU	03 25	4.9	16 03	4.6	09 29	0.7	21 32	1.3
28 M	04 04	4.9	16 41	4.5	10 08	0.8	22 08	1.4
29 TU	04 41	4.8	17 18	4.3	10 44	1.0	22 42	1.5
30 W	05 19	4.6	17 55	4.1	11 21	1.2	23 19	1.7
31 TH	05 59	4.3	18 37	3.9	11 59	1.4	23 59	1.9

Time Zone UT(GMT)

07   SCAVENGER

Blackthorn
Early Spring

Elder
Mid to late Spring

Crab apple
Mid to late Spring

Wild Cherry
Mid to late Spring

Holly
Late Spring to
early Summer

Horse Chestnut
Late Spring to
early Summer

Rowan
Late Spring to early Summer

BEE HOTEL

Objective:
Build a bee hotel to provide a safe nesting spot for pollinating bees.

What You'll Need:
A clean, empty tin can (with both ends removed)
String or twine
Bamboo canes, twigs, or rolled-up paper/cardboard from kitchen rolls
Scissors
Pencil (for rolling paper)

Instructions:
1. Ask an adult to clean the tin can and remove both ends. Make sure there are no sharp edges to avoid cuts.
2. Cut a length of string or twine and thread it through the can. Tie a secure knot to create a loop for hanging later.
3. If using bamboo canes or twigs, cut them to fit snugly inside the can. Ensure they are clean. If using paper or cardboard, fold it to size and wrap it tightly around a pencil to form tubes. These create perfect little homes for bees.
4. Fill the tin can with your materials, packing them tightly so they stay in place.

5. Find a sunny spot in your garden or on a balcony. Hang the hotel where it's sheltered from wind and rain.
6. Take a picture of your bee hotel and share it with friends. Now, patiently wait for bees to move in and make it their home.

Why It's Great:
- Supports local wildlife by providing bees a place to nest
- Encourages observation of bees in your own garden
- Simple and fun project that connects you with nature

Remember:
Always place your bee hotel where it's safe and protected from harsh weather.

LARGE SCALE BEE HOTEL

Objective:
Build a bee hotel from pallets to provide pollinators with a safe place to nest while recycling materials.

What You'll Need:
Wooden pallets (2-3)
Hammer and nails or screws and a screwdriver
Saw
Bamboo canes, twigs, logs, or drilled wood blocks
Straw, pine cones, and other natural materials
Wire mesh (optional)
String or twine
Protective gloves
Sandpaper
Tape measure

Instructions:
1. Disassemble the pallets using a hammer or crowbar, remove nails or screws, and smooth the planks with sandpaper to avoid splinters.
2. Build a rectangular frame using pallets (around 50cm x 50cm x 15cm) using the pallet planks, securing the corners with nails or screws.
3. Add dividers inside the frame to create compartments for different nesting materials.

4. Prepare the filling:
1. Bamboo canes: Cut to fit the compartments and ensure they are hollow and debris-free.
2. Logs/wood blocks: Drill holes (2mm-10mm) to create nesting sites.
3. Twigs/straw: Gather twigs, pinecones, and straw for other compartments.
5. Fill each compartment tightly with the materials, using wire mesh if needed to hold smaller items in place.
7. Hang or position your bee hotel in a sunny, sheltered spot, ideally facing south or southeast, protected from wind and rain.

Why It's Great:
- Recycles old pallets into a habitat for bees
- Helps support local pollinators and biodiversity
- Provides nesting spaces for various bee species

Remember:
Secure your bee hotel firmly, and ensure it's placed in a safe, sunny location to attract as many bees as possible.

NOTES

Hello,
August

08 AUGUST

August arrives in Scotland with the lingering warmth of summer, a month that feels both full and ripe, yet with the first whispers of autumn in the air.

One of the great joys of August is the abundance of fruits and berries that ripen across the countryside. Brambles (blackberries) begin to ripen, hanging in thick clusters along hedgerows and forest edges, just waiting to be picked. Gathering wild brambles, with their deep, sweet flavour, is a simple and rewarding way to connect with nature. Rowan trees are also heavy with their bright red berries, a plant deeply rooted in Scottish folklore. It was traditionally believed that rowan trees offered protection from evil spirits, and their berries were used in various folk remedies. Many households would plant a rowan near their home for good luck and protection.

August is the perfect month to get outdoors and enjoy the height of summer. Whether you're picking brambles along a country lane, walking through the golden fields, or enjoying a day by the coast, nature is at its most generous. The warm days and cool evenings make every outdoor adventure feel rewarding, and you'll find yourself deeply connected to the rhythms of nature as summer quietly begins to fade into autumn.

08 THE MONTH

4th	Owl Day
11th	National Allotments Week
19th	National Photography Day
30th	Toasted Marshmallow Day

Could Do This Month...

♡ _____
♡ _____
♡ _____
♡ _____
♡ _____
♡ _____
♡ _____

08 GARDENING

August kicks off the harvest season, celebrating nature's bounty. Traditionally marked by Lammas (Lughnasadh), a festival honouring the Celtic god Lugh, this time was for feasting and giving thanks for the harvest. Though the formal celebration may have faded, the spirit of abundance endures.

Fields and gardens are bursting with ripe tomatoes, courgettes, beans, and potatoes. It's a great month to enjoy fresh produce, whether picking from your garden or visiting a farmers' market.

Focus on weeding this month, especially if you've had a summer break. Kids can help with this task. Start sowing winter vegetables like spinach, winter onions, and lettuce. Harvest beans, tomatoes, courgettes, onions, and potatoes. Consider a fun project like a "Big Spud Watch" to explore different ways to enjoy your harvest.

08 NIGHT SKY

The Full Moon – August 7, 2025
This Full Moon is often called the Sturgeon Moon, as it coincides with the traditional fishing season for sturgeon in North America.

Throughout the Month
Throughout the summer, the Milky Way stretches across the sky, giving a great view.

The Perseid Meteor Shower – peak around August 12, 2025
One of the most popular and active meteor showers, with up to 150 meteors per hour under ideal conditions. Although the Moon will be in a waning gibbous phase, it might still affect visibility, but the Perseids remain a highlight of the month for stargazers

The Moon Phases

First Quarter	1st August
Full Moon	9th August
Last Quarter	16th August
New Moon	22nd August
First Quarter	31st August

08 WILDLIFE

In August, meadows burst with vibrant colours as knapweed, thistles, and yarrow create a tapestry of purples, yellows, and whites. Bees busily gather the last nectar of the season. Fields are heavy with ripening grain, shimmering with golden hues under the late summer light.

In the woodlands, the canopy remains lush, but hints of autumn start to show as some leaves turn yellow or brown. The bracken is at its fullest, creating a deep green carpet on the forest floor, and ferns and wildflowers fill the undergrowth.

Along Scotland's coast, August offers a rich display of marine life. Seals are commonly seen lounging on rocky shores, while dolphins play in the surf. Seabirds like puffins and guillemots prepare to leave their nesting grounds. The sea is at its warmest, making it an excellent time for coastal walks and boat trips to explore the rugged beauty of the cliffs and islands. Dragonflies and damselflies are active around ponds and lochs, and black grouse are more visible in moorlands and woodland edges. The changing season offers a chance to enjoy the diverse and lively natural world before autumn fully arrives.

08   GARDEN LIFE

In August, your garden in Scotland remains a vibrant haven of activity as summer gradually winds down. The garden is a flurry of colour and motion, with butterflies like small tortoiseshells and red admirals still gracing the scene. These butterflies are drawn to late-summer blooms, such as asters and sedums, which offer a rich supply of nectar. The warm hues of these flowers create a picturesque backdrop for their graceful fluttering.

Birds, on the other hand, are entering a period of moult. This process makes them less conspicuous as they shed old feathers and grow new ones. Despite their diminished visibility, many birds still make occasional visits to feeders in search of an easy meal. Their presence, though less frequent, adds a touch of life to the garden, and you might spot some species, like robins or tits, making a quick stop.

Hedgehogs are particularly active in August, busily foraging for insects, slugs, and other small creatures. Their preparation for the approaching cooler months involves building up fat reserves, so they can continue their nightly excursions with purpose and energy. You might see them rustling through undergrowth or exploring garden nooks, always on the lookout for their next meal.

08   FORAGING

Blackberry

To identify blackberries (Rubus fruticosus) for foraging, look for their dark purple to black, plump, and shiny berries that grow in clusters on thorny, arching canes. The berries are composed of small drupelets and should be juicy and sweet when ripe. The leaves of the blackberry plant are serrated, typically with three or five leaflets, and the stems are covered in sharp, curved thorns.

Blackberries are commonly found in hedgerows, woodland edges, along paths, and in open fields. They thrive in sunny areas but can also grow in partial shade, often forming dense thickets.

The best time to forage blackberries is from late summer to early autumn, typically from August to October. Ripe blackberries are dark in colour and come off the stem easily, while unripe berries are red or green and should be left to ripen.

When foraging, pick the berries carefully to avoid the thorns and gently pull them from the stem. Avoid berries growing near roadsides or areas that may have been sprayed with chemicals.

08 COOKING

Blackberry Oxymel

An oxymel is a traditional herbal preparation that combines vinegar and honey to create a tangy, sweet, and medicinal syrup. Blackberries, with their rich flavour and high vitamin content, are perfect for this.

Ingredients:

1 cup fresh blackberries (or more if you want a larger batch)
1/2 cup raw honey
1/2 cup apple cider vinegar (organic, unfiltered if possible)
A sterilised jar with a lid

Instructions:

1. Rinse the blackberries thoroughly and place them in a sterilised jar.
2. Pour the apple cider vinegar over the blackberries, ensuring the berries are completely submerged.
3. Add the raw honey to the jar. You can stir the mixture to help dissolve the honey, or seal the jar and give it a good shake. You may want to add some greaseproof paper to separate the lid from the contents.
4. Seal the jar tightly and store it in a cool, dark place for 2-4 weeks. Shake the jar every couple of days to mix the contents and help the blackberries release their juices into the vinegar and honey.

5. After 2-4 weeks, strain the mixture through a fine sieve or cheesecloth into a clean jar or bottle, pressing the berries to extract all the liquid.
6. Store the strained oxymel in the fridge, where it will keep for up to 6 months.

How to Use Blackberry Oxymel:
- Take it by the spoonful as an immune-boosting tonic.
- Mix 1-2 tablespoons with sparkling water or still water for a refreshing drink.
- Drizzle it over salads or roasted vegetables as a sweet and tangy dressing.
- Use it as a cocktail mixer with gin or vodka for a herbal twist.

This Blackberry Oxymel is a flavourful way to incorporate the benefits of honey, vinegar, and foraged blackberries into your diet!

08 THE SEA

Date		HEIGHTS ABOVE CHART DATUM							
		High Water				Low Water			
		Morning		Afternoon		Morning		Afternoon	
		Time	m	Time	m	Time	m	Time	m
1	TU	05 59	4.4	18 45	4.0			12 06	1.2
2	W ☽	06 48	4.2	19 34	3.8	00 08	1.9	12 55	1.4
3	TH	07 40	4.0	20 28	3.7	01 00	2.0	13 45	1.6
4	F	08 39	3.8	21 27	3.7	02 00	2.1	14 42	1.8
5	SA	09 46	3.8	22 30	3.7	03 07	2.2	15 44	1.9
6	SU	10 55	3.8	23 27	3.9	04 20	2.1	16 46	1.9
7	M	11 55	3.9			05 21	2.0	17 38	1.8
8	TU	00 16	4.0	12 45	4.0	06 09	1.8	18 20	1.7
9	W	00 57	4.2	13 28	4.1	06 49	1.6	19 00	1.6
10	TH ○	01 36	4.4	14 07	4.3	07 27	1.4	19 38	1.5
11	F	02 11	4.5	14 45	4.4	08 05	1.2	20 15	1.4
12	SA	02 46	4.6	15 23	4.5	08 44	1.0	20 54	1.3
13	SU	03 21	4.7	16 02	4.5	09 23	0.9	21 32	1.3
14	M	03 59	4.7	16 41	4.5	10 04	0.9	22 12	1.3
15	TU	04 37	4.7	17 23	4.4	10 45	0.9	22 52	1.4
16	W	05 20	4.7	18 09	4.3	11 30	1.0	23 38	1.5
17	TH	06 07	4.6	19 00	4.2			12 18	1.1
18	F ☾	07 02	4.5	19 59	4.1	00 32	1.7	13 15	1.3
19	SA	08 08	4.3	21 05	4.0	01 35	1.8	14 18	1.5
20	SU	09 22	4.2	22 16	4.0	02 47	1.8	15 29	1.6
21	M	10 43	4.2	23 26	4.2	04 06	1.8	16 47	1.6
22	TU	11 59	4.3			05 23	1.5	17 53	1.6
23	W	00 27	4.4	13 02	4.5	06 23	1.3	18 46	1.5
24	TH ●	01 18	4.6	13 55	4.6	07 17	1.0	19 34	1.4
25	F	02 03	4.8	14 41	4.7	08 04	0.8	20 16	1.3
26	SA	02 45	4.9	15 23	4.7	08 49	0.7	20 56	1.3
27	SU	03 25	4.9	16 03	4.6	09 29	0.7	21 32	1.3
28	M	04 04	4.9	16 41	4.5	10 08	0.8	22 08	1.4
29	TU	04 41	4.8	17 18	4.3	10 44	1.0	22 42	1.5
30	W	05 19	4.6	17 55	4.1	11 21	1.2	23 19	1.7
31	TH	05 59	4.3	18 37	3.9	11 59	1.4	23 59	1.9

08   SCAVENGER

Hear
Something that makes a noise

See
Something with more than 1 colour

Touch
Something that feels smooth

Smell
Somethingh that smells pleasant

Taste
Something an animal could eat

EDIBLE PLANTS

Edible Flower*	Tastes Like	Which Parts are Edible?	Best Eaten In/With
Calendula	Peppery citrus	Petals	Salads, stir fry, coleslaw, biscuits
Carnation	Peppery clove	Petals	Salads, meats, cheesecake
Hollyhock	Mild marshmallow	Petals, leaves and roots	Garnish, salad dressing
Lavender	Mild sweetness	Flowers	Biscuits, tea, cakes, ice cream
Nasturtium	Peppery watercress	Whole flower and leaves	Salad, stir fry, pasta
Pansy	Lettuce	Whole Flower	Garnish, salad, sandwich, fruit salad
Sunflower	Nutty	Buds, petals and seeds	Bread, biscuits, cakes
Viola	Mild sweetness	Whole Flower	Garnish, salad, sandwich, cake decoration

*If you have asthma or allergies take caution when eating edible flowers and only try a small amount.

PHOTOGRAPH HABITATS

Objective:
Explore and understand local wildlife and habitats through research, outdoor exploration, and creative presentations.

Materials Needed:
Research materials (books, online resources)
Digital cameras/smartphones
Computers/tablets with internet access
Art supplies (paper, markers)

Instructions:
1. Discuss biodiversity and local animals. Brainstorm types of wildlife they might see, such as birds, mammals, or insects.
2. Divide children into groups and assign an animal or group of animals to research. Guide them in finding information on habitats, homes, and behaviours.
3. Take children outside to observe animal signs like nests, burrows, or tracks. Use cameras to capture any signs of wildlife.
4. Return indoors and help children create factsheets on their assigned animals, including habitat, signs of presence, and needs. Encourage creativity with images and drawings.

5. Each group presents their factsheets, sharing their findings and fostering discussion with classmates.
6. Reflect on what was learned about local wildlife and biodiversity, discussing how to protect and preserve local ecosystems.

Why It's Great:
- Encourages outdoor exploration and observation, fostering a deeper connection to nature.
- Teaches valuable research skills and creativity through factsheet creation.
- Promotes teamwork and peer learning through group work and presentations.

Remember:
- Encourage children to explore respectfully without disturbing wildlife or habitats.
- This activity not only teaches about local animals but also helps children understand the importance of biodiversity and how they can help protect it.

NOTES

Hello,
September

09 SEPTEMBER

September in Scotland marks a beautiful turning point, as the landscape begins its gentle shift from summer's bounty to autumn's cooler embrace. The mornings are crisper, the days shorter, and the first signs of change are all around. September is a month of richness, not just in terms of harvest but in the subtle changes that signal autumn's approach. It's a time to get outside and witness the magic of the season's quiet transformation.

In Scotland's lochs and rivers, September marks the start of the salmon run. Atlantic salmon, having spent years in the ocean, return to their freshwater breeding grounds, leaping upstream in a dramatic display of strength and perseverance.

Scottish folklore also reminds us of the importance of this transitional month. Known as the time of the autumn equinox, or Mabon, September was celebrated as a time of balance, when day and night were equal. It was a moment to give thanks for the harvest and reflect on the coming darker months. Many believed that this balance between light and dark also reflected a balance between the physical and spiritual worlds, with September carrying a quiet sense of reflection and gratitude.

09 THE MONTH

2nd	European Bike Week
6th	Read a Book Day
8th	International Literacy Day
16th	International Preservation of the Ozone Layer Day
19th	Youth Mental Health Day
20th (to 29th)	Big British Beach Clean
21st	FSC Forest Week
22nd	Autumn Equinox
23rd	Seed Gathering Fortnight
	Maths Week Scotland
26th	European Languages Day
27th	Doodle Day
28th	World Rivers Day

Could Do This Month...

♡ _____
♡ _____
♡ _____
♡ _____
♡ _____
♡ _____
♡ _____

09 GARDENING

One of the most noticeable changes in September is the hedgerows bursting with fruit. The brambles (blackberries) that ripened in August are now at their sweetest, while rosehips and sloes hang like jewels, ready to be picked. Elderberries, dark and glossy, weigh down the branches, inviting foragers to gather them for syrups and wines. This is the perfect time to take a walk and enjoy nature's bounty, whether you're gathering fruit for jams or simply savouring the experience of being out in the fresh air.

Lots of my beds will be empty this month so I am making sure to clear them all and compost them. Any beds still producing still need weeding.

I can sow my lambs lettuce and indoors salad (this can even be on a class windowsill).

I can plant my spinach as well as onion, and lettuce. Harvest wise, there can be lots! Just have a look at all your summer crops to see which are ready to come in.

09 NIGHT SKY

Moon at Apogee - September 26, 2025,
This means the Moon will be at its farthest distance from Earth during its orbit, about 404,000 kilometres away. While this doesn't lead to any dramatic changes to the naked eye, the Moon will appear slightly smaller in the night sky compared to other phases.

Full Moon in September - September 7, 2025
This Full Moon is also significant because it coincides with a total lunar eclipse, adding to the spectacle for observers. This Full Moon is often called the Harvest Moon, marking the closest full moon to the autumn equinox.

The Moon Phases

Full Moon	7th September
Last Quarter	14th September
New Moon	21st September
First Quarter	30th September

09 WILDLIFE

In September, wildlife is bustling with preparations for the colder months. Squirrels are actively gathering nuts and seeds, darting around woodlands and rustling through leaves as they stock up for winter. Their busy activity is a vivid reminder of nature's rhythms and seasonal changes.

The skies are also transitioning. Swallows and house martins, which have been a summer staple, start to gather in large groups, signalling their imminent migration south. Their presence, along with the honking calls of migrating geese arriving from the Arctic, marks the changing season.

In addition, red deer stags enter their rutting season, and their powerful roars echo through the Highlands and Cairngorms. September is also a peak time for spotting migrating geese in Scotland, with flocks populating wetlands and coastal areas like Loch Leven and the Solway Firth. Red squirrels, particularly active in places like Perthshire and Aberdeenshire, are foraging intensively as they prepare for winter.

09 GARDEN LIFE

In September, your garden in Scotland undergoes a noticeable transition as the early signs of autumn begin to emerge. As the days shorten and temperatures cool, birds that have been less active during their summer moult start to make a more frequent appearance at feeders. Species like robins, tits, and finches become increasingly visible, flocking to feeders to replenish their energy reserves. This is a perfect time to observe their changing behaviours and enjoy their lively presence.

Hedgehogs, too, become more conspicuous as they work diligently to gather food and build up their fat reserves for hibernation. Providing supplementary food such as cat food or specialised hedgehog food can support these nocturnal foragers during this crucial time.

If you have fruiting trees or bushes, you'll likely notice an increase in activity among small mammals and birds, all eager to take advantage of the harvest. Squirrels may be seen darting about, collecting and storing nuts, while various bird species feast on the fruits and berries.

09 FORAGING

Heather Flowers

To identify heather flowers (Calluna vulgaris) for foraging, look for their small, bell-shaped flowers that range in colour from pale pink to purple. The flowers grow in dense spikes along slender, woody stems, and the plant itself has tiny, scale-like leaves that give it a bushy appearance. Heather is a low-growing shrub that forms dense patches, often carpeting large areas of moorland or heath.

Heather is commonly found in open, acidic soils such as moorlands, heathlands, and peat bogs. It thrives in well-drained areas and is a familiar sight in the Scottish Highlands and other upland regions of the UK.

The best time to forage for heather flowers is in late summer, from August to September, when the plant is in full bloom. The flowers are fragrant and can be collected by gently plucking the flowering tops, taking care not to damage the plant.

When foraging, pick the flower spikes in moderation, leaving plenty for the plant to regenerate and for wildlife to use. Heather flowers can be used to make teas, infused honey, syrups, and even in baking to add a subtle, floral flavour.

09 COOKING

Heather Flower Syrup

Heather syrup is a fragrant, floral sweetener that can be used in teas, desserts, or cocktails.

Ingredients:
1 cup fresh or dried heather flowers
1 cup sugar
1 cup water

Instructions:
1. Combine the sugar and water in a saucepan and bring to a gentle simmer, stirring until the sugar is dissolved.
2. Add the heather flowers and simmer for about 10 minutes.
3. Remove from heat and let the syrup steep for an additional 20-30 minutes.
4. Strain the flowers and store the syrup in a sterilised bottle in the fridge.

09 THE SEA

Date		HEIGHTS ABOVE CHART DATUM						
		High Water				Low Water			
		Morning		Afternoon		Morning		Afternoon	
		Time	m	Time	m	Time	m	Time	m
1	M	08 01	3.6	20 33	3.6	01 00	2.3	13 44	2.4
2	TU	09 28	3.5	21 56	3.7	02 37	2.4	15 21	2.4
3	W	11 01	3.7	23 14	3.9	04 27	2.2	16 50	2.3
4	TH			12 04	3.9	05 26	1.9	17 40	2.0
5	F	00 08	4.2	12 48	4.3	06 08	1.5	18 19	1.7
6	SA	00 50	4.5	13 25	4.5	06 44	1.2	18 56	1.4
7	SU ○	01 25	4.8	14 00	4.8	07 21	0.9	19 32	1.2
8	M	02 00	5.1	14 35	5.0	07 58	0.6	20 08	1.0
9	TU	02 35	5.3	15 11	5.0	08 35	0.5	20 46	0.9
10	W	03 12	5.4	15 48	5.0	09 14	0.5	21 23	0.9
11	TH	03 52	5.3	16 26	4.8	09 52	0.6	22 03	1.0
12	F	04 35	5.1	17 09	4.6	10 34	0.9	22 47	1.3
13	SA	05 24	4.8	17 58	4.4	11 20	1.3	23 42	1.5
14	SU ☾	06 24	4.4	19 01	4.1			12 18	1.8
15	M	07 44	4.1	20 21	3.9	00 55	1.8	13 37	2.2
16	TU	09 19	3.9	21 51	3.9	02 32	1.9	15 22	2.3
17	W	10 58	4.0	23 13	4.2	04 14	1.7	16 49	2.1
18	TH			12 06	4.3	05 21	1.4	17 42	1.9
19	F	00 11	4.5	12 53	4.5	06 11	1.2	18 24	1.7
20	SA	00 54	4.7	13 30	4.6	06 51	1.0	19 00	1.5
21	SU ●	01 31	4.9	14 01	4.7	07 27	0.9	19 33	1.3
22	M	02 03	5.0	14 31	4.7	07 59	0.8	20 04	1.2
23	TU	02 34	5.0	14 59	4.7	08 29	0.9	20 33	1.2
24	W	03 06	4.9	15 27	4.7	08 58	1.0	21 03	1.3
25	TH	03 36	4.8	15 56	4.6	09 26	1.1	21 31	1.4
26	F	04 09	4.6	16 25	4.4	09 53	1.4	22 02	1.5
27	SA	04 43	4.4	16 59	4.3	10 24	1.6	22 37	1.7
28	**SU**	05 24	4.1	17 37	4.1	10 59	1.9	23 20	2.0
29	M ☽	06 14	3.8	18 30	3.8	11 44	2.2		
30	TU	07 26	3.6	19 45	3.7	00 20	2.2	12 55	2.5

Time Zone UT(GMT)

09   SCAVENGER

Find an object in nature or your environment for each letter of the alphabet, encouraging exploration, observation, and creativity.

What You'll Need:
- A notepad or alphabet sheet
- A pen or pencil
- A camera (optional, to document your findings)

Instructions:
1. Start by writing out the alphabet from A to Z on a sheet of paper or in a notebook.
2. Head outside to a garden, park, woodland, or any outdoor space. You can also adapt this for indoor environments like a school or home.
3. Begin hunting for objects that correspond to each letter of the alphabet. You can be creative—objects can be plants, animals, colours, or even shapes.
   - For example, 'A' could be an acorn, 'B' could be bark, 'C' could be clover, and so on.
4. If you can't find a specific item for a letter, think outside the box. Perhaps 'Q' can be a "quiet spot," or 'X' can represent an 'X-shaped' twig.

MINDFUL LISTENING

Objective:
Develop listening skills and creativity by mapping nature's sounds.

Instructions:
1. Gather students outdoors, explaining they'll observe and record nature's sounds, focusing on attentive listening.
2. Provide paper and drawing tools. Have students sit quietly, close their eyes, and map sounds using symbols like circles or waves. Clipboards can help manage materials.
3. Gather students to share their sound maps, discussing the variety of sounds they noticed.
4. Reflect on how sound mapping heightened their awareness of nature and encourage continued exploration.

Why It's Great:
- Enhances observation skills
- Fosters creativity through sound representation
- Deepens connection with nature
- Promotes mindfulness

Remember:
- Listen carefully to connect with nature.
- Be creative with your sound map; it's personal to your experience.

FIBONACCI IN NATURE

Objective:
Explore the Fibonacci sequence and its presence in nature through calculation, observation, and pattern recognition.

Instructions:
1. Explain the Fibonacci sequence (1, 1, 2, 3, 5, 8...) and its importance in math and nature.
2. In small groups, calculate the first six Fibonacci numbers and discuss the pattern.
3. Explore outdoor areas to find natural patterns, like branching or petal arrangements, that match the Fibonacci sequence. Discuss any deviations observed.
4. Introduce the golden ratio, show natural spirals (e.g., seashells, pinecones), and demonstrate their connection to the Fibonacci sequence.
5. Recap key concepts, emphasising the Fibonacci sequence's significance in nature and encouraging students to observe patterns in their surroundings.

Why It's Great:
- Enhances math understanding
- Connects math with nature
- Encourages observation and critical thinking

Remember:
- The Fibonacci sequence is all around—watch for patterns and spirals.
- Appreciate nature's beauty through its mathematical structure.
- Consider why some patterns deviate; nature is diverse and complex.

NOTES

Hello, October

10 OCTOBER

In Scotland, October fully embraces autumn, painting the landscape with vibrant reds, oranges, and golds. The crisp air and shorter days bring a rich, transformative feel. Trees, from beech to oak, don their fiery autumn leaves, creating a stunning contrast with the deep green pines and yews. Walking through the forest is a sensory delight with crunching leaves and earthy smells.

October's folklore is rich with the mystical, as the month leads into Samhain, the ancient Celtic festival marking the end of the harvest and the beginning of winter. It was believed that the veil between the physical world and the spirit world was at its thinnest during this time, allowing spirits to pass through. Many of today's Halloween traditions, such as carving pumpkins or turnips, dressing in costumes, and lighting bonfires, are rooted in these ancient customs.

Despite the cooler weather, October rewards outdoor exploration. Bundle up and enjoy the last blaze of autumn, whether by exploring colourful forests, listening to migrating geese, or simply relaxing by a loch. This month is perfect for experiencing the beauty of change.

10 THE MONTH

Popcorn Poppin' Month
International Walk to School Month

2nd	Yom Kippur
	Poetry Day
4th	World Animal Day
	Fungus Day
	World Space Week
6th	Badger Day
	World Habitat Day
10th	Forest School Day
	World Mental Health Day
12th	world Migrartory Bird Day
13th	National Mammal Week
21st	International Apple Day
24th	Bat Appreciate Week
31st	Halloween

Could Do This Month...

♡ _____
♡ _____
♡ _____
♡ _____
♡ _____
♡ _____
♡ _____

10 GARDENING

As October rolls in, the vast majority of my garden beds will be empty, making it the perfect time to give them some much-needed TLC. Weeding, clearing out old plants, and adding compost will ensure the soil is nourished and ready for future planting. This maintenance is essential for keeping the beds in top condition, helping to suppress weeds, and enriching the earth for the next growing season.

I can sow garlic and broad beans now, which will be ready to harvest early next year. These hardy crops thrive in the cooler months, making them ideal for autumn planting. It's also a good time to plant out sprouts, beans, cucumbers, and tomatoes, as they'll benefit from the milder temperatures and will establish themselves before winter sets in. Towards the end of the month, I'll be planting swede and leek, which will mature through the colder months.

When it comes to harvesting, October can be quite rewarding! There's still plenty of summer produce that may be ready to bring in. By checking on crops like tomatoes, cucumbers, and beans, I can ensure I make the most of what the garden has left to offer before the frosts arrive. Don't forget to inspect each bed to see what's ripened and ready to enjoy.

10 NIGHT SKY

Full Moon in October 2025 - October 6, 2025
This Full Moon is often referred to as the Hunter's Moon, marking the time of year when hunting traditionally took place to prepare for winter.

Orionid Meteor Shower - active until October 26, 2025
While the peak of the Orionid meteor shower occurs earlier in the month (around October 21), it remains active until October 26. The meteors are fragments from Halley's Comet and are best viewed in the predawn hours

The Moon Phases

Full Moon	7th October
Last Quarter	13th October
New Moon	21st October
First Quarter	29th October

10 WILDLIFE

October's woodlands are alive with fungi, as mushrooms and toadstools of various shapes and colours emerge. Fly agaric, with its bright red cap and white spots, stands out, while chanterelles, puffballs, and wood blewits can be found beneath logs and along the forest floor. Foragers enjoy the bounty, but caution is advised with poisonous varieties, making simple mushroom-spotting a pleasure in itself.

In the skies, summer birds have migrated, replaced by winter visitors like redwings and fieldfares from Scandinavia. Geese continue to arrive, filling the skies with their calls as they settle on lochs and wetlands. These gatherings, especially in morning mist or at sunset, are peaceful reminders of nature's cycles.

October also marks the red deer rutting season, with stags' deep bellows echoing across hills and glens. Watching their dramatic battles is one of Scotland's most powerful wildlife experiences. In rivers like the Tay and Tweed, salmon leap upstream to their spawning grounds, a striking natural event to witness.

10   GARDEN LIFE

In October, your garden fully embraces the beauty of autumn as the season settles in. The leaves on trees like maples, oaks, and birches transform into a tapestry of vibrant reds, oranges, and yellows, creating a striking autumnal backdrop. This burst of colour is complemented by the lively activity of wildlife preparing for the colder months ahead.

Birds such as robins, blackbirds, and thrushes become more visible, busily foraging for berries from rowan and hawthorn trees. Their songs and fluttering movements bring a sense of energy to the garden, as they stock up on food before winter arrives. Squirrels can be spotted darting about, gathering nuts and acorns to store for the months ahead, while hedgehogs are often seen foraging for insects and slugs, building up the fat reserves they need to hibernate successfully.

October is a month of preparation for the wildlife in your garden. As animals and insects gather food and ready themselves for winter, your garden becomes a bustling hub of activity, showcasing the resilience and beauty of nature's changing rhythms.

10   FORAGING

Rowan Berries

To identify rowan berries (Sorbus aucuparia) for foraging, look for clusters of small, bright red or orange berries that grow on a deciduous tree with pinnate leaves. The leaves are made up of multiple narrow, toothed leaflets arranged in pairs along a central stem. Rowan trees are relatively small and slender, with smooth, greyish bark. The berries appear in dense clusters and ripen from late summer to autumn.

Rowan trees are commonly found in woodlands, along hedgerows, and in upland areas. They thrive in well-drained soil and are often planted in parks and gardens as ornamental trees.

The best time to forage for rowan berries is from late August through October when the berries are fully ripe and brightly coloured. It's recommended to harvest after the first frost, as this helps to reduce the bitterness in the berries. If foraging before the frost, you can also freeze the berries for a day or two to achieve the same effect.

10 COOKING

Rowan Berry Jelly

This is one of the most common ways to use rowan berries, creating a tart, sweet jelly that's perfect with meats, cheese, or on toast.

Ingredients:
1 kg rowan berries (after the first frost, or freeze them to reduce bitterness)
1 kg apples (for natural pectin)
1.5 litres water
Sugar (about 500g per 500ml of juice)

Instructions:
1. Wash the rowan berries and apples, then roughly chop the apples (no need to peel or core).
2. Place the berries and apples in a large pot, cover with water, and simmer for about an hour until soft.
3. Strain the mixture through a muslin cloth or jelly bag overnight to collect the juice.
4. Measure the juice, and for every 500ml of juice, add 500g of sugar.
5. Bring the juice and sugar to a boil and simmer until it reaches a setting point (use a cold plate to test).
6. Pour into sterilised jars and seal. Store in a cool, dark place.

10 THE SEA

Date	HEIGHTS ABOVE CHART DATUM						
	High Water				Low Water			
	Morning		Afternoon		Morning		Afternoon	
	Time	m	Time	m	Time	m	Time	m
1 W	08 51	3.6	21 08	3.7	01 54	2.3	14 40	2.5
2 TH	10 21	3.7	22 30	3.9	03 40	2.2	16 12	2.4
3 F	11 28	4.0	23 29	4.2	04 49	1.8	17 08	2.0
4 SA			12 15	4.3	05 33	1.5	17 48	1.7
5 SU	00 14	4.5	12 53	4.7	06 12	1.1	18 25	1.4
6 M	00 52	4.9	13 29	4.9	06 50	0.8	19 03	1.1
7 TU ○	01 30	5.2	14 05	5.1	07 28	0.6	19 41	0.9
8 W	02 08	5.4	14 42	5.2	08 06	0.5	20 19	0.8
9 TH	02 50	5.5	15 20	5.1	08 47	0.6	21 01	0.8
10 F	03 33	5.4	16 01	5.0	09 27	0.8	21 44	1.0
11 SA	04 21	5.1	16 45	4.7	10 12	1.2	22 35	1.2
12 SU	05 15	4.7	17 36	4.4	11 01	1.6	23 36	1.5
13 M ☾	06 22	4.3	18 44	4.2			12 04	2.0
14 TU	07 44	4.0	20 06	4.0	00 54	1.7	13 29	2.4
15 W	09 17	3.9	21 33	4.0	02 30	1.8	15 10	2.4
16 TH	10 46	4.0	22 51	4.2	03 59	1.6	16 27	2.2
17 F	11 45	4.2	23 47	4.4	05 01	1.4	17 18	2.0
18 SA			12 28	4.4	05 46	1.3	17 59	1.8
19 SU	00 29	4.6	13 03	4.5	06 23	1.1	18 33	1.6
20 M	01 05	4.7	13 32	4.6	06 57	1.1	19 06	1.4
21 TU ●	01 37	4.8	14 01	4.7	07 27	1.1	19 37	1.3
22 W	02 08	4.8	14 28	4.7	07 56	1.1	20 07	1.3
23 TH	02 40	4.8	14 56	4.7	08 24	1.2	20 37	1.3
24 F	03 12	4.7	15 24	4.6	08 54	1.3	21 07	1.4
25 SA	03 45	4.5	15 55	4.5	09 22	1.5	21 39	1.5
26 SU	04 22	4.3	16 27	4.4	09 54	1.7	22 16	1.7
27 M	05 02	4.1	17 06	4.2	10 30	2.0	23 00	1.9
28 TU	05 52	3.9	17 55	4.0	11 17	2.2	23 59	2.0
29 W ☽	06 59	3.7	19 04	3.8			12 23	2.4
30 TH	08 15	3.7	20 23	3.8	01 18	2.1	13 53	2.5
31 F	09 32	3.8	21 35	4.0	02 45	2.0	15 18	2.3

Time Zone UT(GMT)

10 SCAVENGER

Black Cat	 Spider Web	 Creepy Branch	 Carved Pumpkin
 Bat	 Ghost	 Skeleton	 Witches Hat
 Candle	 Broomstick	Gravestone	The Number 13
 Owl	 Potion Bottle	 Cauldron	 Shadow

SENSORY BAREFOOT WALK

Objective:
Connect with nature and enhance sensory awareness by walking barefoot on various natural textures.

What You'll Need:
Safe, flat outdoor space
Natural materials: pebbles, sand, grass, leaves, mud, bark, etc.
Garden hose or water (optional)

Instructions:
1. Choose a safe, flat outdoor space like a garden or park.
2. Collect natural items like pebbles, sand, grass, leaves, and mud.
3. Mark a path and arrange the materials in sections (e.g., smooth pebbles, soft grass, wet mud).
4. Ensure safety and comfort by removing sharp objects.
5. Remove shoes and slowly walk, focusing on the sensations of each texture.
6. Use a hose or bucket to rinse your feet afterward.
7. Take time to reflect on how the walk affected your senses and mood.

Why It's Great:
- Promotes mindfulness and connection with nature
- Stimulates senses through touch and temperature
- Relaxing and grounding experience for all ages

Remember:
Move at your own pace, adjust as needed, and enjoy the calming experience of walking barefoot in nature.

MAGIC WAND

Materials Needed:

Pens

Paint

Stick

Wool

String Ribbon

Instructions:

1. What does every good fairy carry at all times? Why, a wand of course!
2. So, today we make a wand for your fairies! To begin, find a stick. Now, it cannot be any old stick, you need to find a stick that is just right for casting those spells.
3. Then, decide how you wish to decorate it. You can whittle, paint, draw, wrap in yarn, whatever helps create some magic.
4. Take your time, the more care and attention you give when creating your wand, the more magic will be created by it.
5. Once your wand is complete, it is your job to be responsible. You need to carefully think about the spells you will cast. Be kind and stay safe are the only rules!
6. As always, we want to see your pics. So please, share on the Facebook page!
7. Enjoy making magic

NOTES

Hello,
November

11 NOVEMBER

November marks the true arrival of late autumn, with winter casting its shadow across the landscape. The trees stand bare, the days shorten, and the air carries a sharp bite, but there's a quiet beauty that invites you outdoors.

With the leaves fallen, the trees reveal their intricate structures, silhouetted against the sky. Walking through woodlands, the crunch of leaves underfoot and frost-covered ground create a peaceful atmosphere.

Scottish folklore sees November as a time of reckoning with nature's forces, following Samhain. The Cailleach, the winter goddess, becomes more prominent, symbolising the harshness of the season with cold, storms, and frost. Her presence is felt in the wild weather, shaping the land as winter takes hold.

November is a reflective month. As the natural world slows, the subdued landscapes encourage stillness and mindfulness. Misty mornings and low light create an ethereal atmosphere, making it the perfect time for quiet walks, taking in the muted colours and listening to nature prepare for winter.

11 THE MONTH

5th	Stress Awareness Day
	Bonfire/ Guy Fawkes Night
8th	National STEM Day
10th	Start of COP30
11th	Remembrance Day
13th	World Kindness Day
17th	Global Education Week
	Scottish Book Week
20th	Diwali
21st	Global Outdoor Learning Day
27th	National Tree Week
30th	St Andrew's Day

Could Do This Month...

♡ _____
♡ _____
♡ _____
♡ _____
♡ _____
♡ _____
♡ _____

11   GARDENING

As the year winds down, so does the activity in my garden, with fewer tasks to manage as winter approaches. However, there's still a satisfying harvest to enjoy. My spinach is ready to pick, providing fresh, leafy greens for soups and salads. Parsnips and swedes are at their best now, having benefitted from the cooler temperatures that enhance their sweetness, making them perfect for hearty stews or roasting.

Leeks, which have been growing steadily through the summer, are now ready to be pulled, adding a mild onion flavour to winter dishes. The salad greens offer a crisp, fresh addition to meals, even as the colder weather sets in.

Root vegetables like carrots, beetroot, and turnips can still be harvested, each bringing earthy flavours to the table. These vegetables, which store well, will help sustain my kitchen through the colder months ahead. This late-season harvest, though smaller, is a rewarding culmination of the year's work in the garden.

11 NIGHT SKY

Full Moon – November 5, 2025
The Full Moon will occur on this date, brightening the night sky. It's a great time for lunar observation, especially with clear skies.

Leonid Meteor Shower – November 17, 2025
The Leonid meteor shower will peak on this night, potentially offering up to 15 meteors per hour. This shower is known for producing bright meteors with persistent trails, making it a highlight of November skywatching.

Conjunction of the Moon and Mars – November 21, 2025
The Moon and Mars will appear very close to each other in the sky, creating a striking visual spectacle. This conjunction will be visible in the evening sky

The Moon Phases

Full Moon	5th November
Last Quarter	12th November
New Moon	20th November
First Quarter	28th November

11 WILDLIFE

By this time, many animals have either migrated or settled into their winter routines. Red squirrels are busy storing the last of their nuts, while hedgehogs have now entered hibernation. If you're lucky, you might spot a red squirrel darting through the branches, its bright fur standing out against the greys and browns of the trees. While wildlife may seem quieter, there's still much to observe—roe deer, often shy and elusive, are more visible as they move through the fields and woodlands, and birds like robins and blackbirds remain active, providing bursts of life as they forage for food.

On the coast, November brings its own rugged beauty. The sea, now colder and wilder, crashes against rocky cliffs and empty beaches. Grey seals, which started their pupping season in September, are still active along the shorelines. If you visit a quiet cove or coastal path, you might spot seal pups resting on the beaches, their soft white fur standing out against the dark sands. The colder, quieter coastlines offer a sense of isolation and raw beauty that is uniquely rewarding for those willing to explore.

11 GARDEN LIFE

In November, your Scottish garden becomes a quieter, more reflective space as wildlife makes its final preparations for winter. Birds like robins, blackbirds, and blue tits are frequent visitors, drawn to feeders stocked with high-energy foods such as seeds, suet, and peanuts. These foods provide much-needed sustenance as they gear up for colder, harsher days. It's a good idea to keep feeders clean and topped up regularly, as your garden birds will rely on them more as natural food sources diminish.

Hedgehogs may still be active in the evenings if they haven't yet begun hibernating. If you have a pile of fallen leaves, consider leaving them in place, as they create excellent shelter for both hedgehogs and beneficial insects like ladybirds and beetles. This natural mulch also protects the soil, adding nutrients as it decomposes.

Squirrels remain busy, burying nuts and seeds to store for the winter months. You may spot them darting around the garden, foraging and preparing their caches for the colder season.

11 FORAGING

Hazelnuts

To identify hazelnuts (Corylus avellana) for foraging, look for their small, round, or oval nuts encased in a green, leafy husk. The nuts grow in clusters on a bushy deciduous shrub called the hazel tree. Hazel trees have broad, rounded leaves with serrated edges and a slightly fuzzy texture. In autumn, the husks turn brown as the nuts ripen.

Hazel trees are commonly found in woodlands, hedgerows, and sometimes in open fields. They prefer well-drained soils and can grow in both sunny and partially shaded areas.

When the nuts are fully mature and start to drop from the trees. Ripe hazelnuts are usually brown, and the leafy husk may begin to peel away naturally. You can collect them by picking them directly from the tree or gathering those that have fallen to the ground.

When foraging, inspect the nuts to ensure they are free of holes or other signs of insects. Hazelnuts can be eaten fresh, but they are best after being dried or roasted to enhance their flavour.

11 COOKING

Roasted Hazelnuts

Roasting hazelnuts brings out their rich, nutty flavour, making them perfect for snacking or adding to other recipes.

Instructions:

1. Preheat the oven to 180°C (350°F).
2. Spread the hazelnuts in a single layer on a baking tray.
3. Roast for 10-15 minutes, shaking the tray halfway through.
4. Once the skins start to crack and the nuts are golden, remove from the oven.
5. To remove the skins, place the hazelnuts in a clean kitchen towel and rub them together to loosen the skins.
6. Store roasted hazelnuts in an airtight container and enjoy them as a snack or chopped up and sprinkled on salads or desserts.

11 THE SEA

Date		High Water Morning Time	m	High Water Afternoon Time	m	Low Water Morning Time	m	Low Water Afternoon Time	m
1	SA	10 41	4.1	22 40	4.2	03 56	1.7	16 21	2.1
2	SU	11 33	4.4	23 32	4.6	04 49	1.4	17 09	1.8
3	M			12 18	4.7	05 34	1.1	17 52	1.5
4	TU	00 18	4.9	12 58	4.9	06 17	0.9	18 33	1.2
5	W ○	01 02	5.2	13 37	5.1	06 59	0.7	19 16	1.0
6	TH	01 47	5.3	14 16	5.2	07 41	0.7	20 00	0.9
7	F	02 32	5.4	14 58	5.1	08 24	0.8	20 46	0.9
8	SA	03 20	5.2	15 41	5.0	09 10	1.1	21 35	0.9
9	SU	04 13	5.0	16 28	4.8	09 58	1.4	22 30	1.1
10	M	05 12	4.7	17 23	4.5	10 50	1.8	23 33	1.3
11	TU	06 19	4.3	18 28	4.3	11 52	2.1		
12	W ☾	07 31	4.1	19 41	4.2	00 45	1.5	13 07	2.3
13	TH	08 48	4.0	20 56	4.1	02 03	1.6	14 28	2.4
14	F	10 06	4.0	22 11	4.2	03 20	1.6	15 44	2.3
15	SA	11 07	4.1	23 10	4.3	04 23	1.6	16 42	2.1
16	SU	11 52	4.2	23 57	4.4	05 11	1.5	17 26	1.9
17	M			12 29	4.4	05 51	1.4	18 05	1.7
18	TU	00 37	4.5	13 02	4.5	06 24	1.4	18 40	1.6
19	W	01 13	4.6	13 32	4.6	06 57	1.4	19 14	1.5
20	TH ●	01 48	4.6	14 01	4.7	07 28	1.4	19 47	1.4
21	F	02 21	4.6	14 32	4.7	07 59	1.4	20 19	1.4
22	SA	02 56	4.5	15 02	4.7	08 30	1.5	20 53	1.5
23	SU	03 31	4.5	15 33	4.6	09 03	1.6	21 28	1.5
24	M	04 08	4.3	16 08	4.5	09 37	1.8	22 07	1.6
25	TU	04 49	4.2	16 47	4.4	10 16	1.9	22 50	1.7
26	W	05 36	4.0	17 33	4.2	11 00	2.1	23 42	1.8
27	TH	06 33	3.9	18 29	4.1	11 56	2.2		
28	F ☽	07 36	3.9	19 36	4.1	00 44	1.8	13 05	2.3
29	SA	08 42	3.9	20 43	4.1	01 53	1.8	14 20	2.2
30	SU	09 48	4.1	21 48	4.3	02 59	1.7	15 27	2.1

Time Zone UT(GMT)

11 SCAVENGER

Beech
Increases sensitivity

Pine
Gives positivity

Larch
Builds confidence

Sycamore
Grants wisdom

Rowan
Inspiration and protection

Oak
Wisdom

Birch
Calms emotions

Ash
Healing

Holly
Peace and goodwill

Aspen
Keeps you safe from harm

Goat Willow
Fresh Starts

Hazel
Increase wisdom and helps communication

MAKE A BOAT

Objective:
Build a boat that floats using various materials to explore buoyancy and problem-solving.

What You'll Need:
A variety of materials (paper, twigs, etc.)
A water container (tub, tray, or stream/pond)
Towels for cleanup
Optional: scissors, tape, glue

Instructions:
1. Explain the challenge: build a boat that floats.
2. Briefly discuss buoyancy and encourage trial and error for improving designs.
3. Let children choose from a variety of materials and brainstorm boat designs.
4. Children build their boats using the materials provided, testing and adjusting their designs as needed.
5. Test boats in the water container, stream, or pond. Adjust as needed to improve floating ability. Ensure you tie a string to them so you can pull them back in. We don't want to litter.
6. Discuss what worked or didn't work. Celebrate creative solutions and efforts.
7. Collect all materials, ensuring no litter is left behind.
8. Reflect on how trial and error led to better designs.

Why It's Great:
- Encourages creativity, experimentation, and problem-solving.
- Teaches basic buoyancy principles through hands-on learning.

Remember:
- Allow trial and error for learning.
- Collect materials to avoid littering.
- Celebrate all designs, whether they float or not.

STEM STICK TOWER

Objective:
Build the tallest tower using sticks to explore creativity, balance, and problem-solving.

What You'll Need:
Sticks of various lengths (gathered from outdoors)
Optional: string, tape, or twine to secure connections
Flat surface for building

Instructions:
1. Explain the challenge: build the tallest tower using only sticks. Discuss the importance of balance, structure, and stability.
2. Allow children to choose their sticks and brainstorm ideas for how to make their towers tall and stable.
3. Children start building their towers using the materials provided, experimenting with different designs to create a stable structure.
4. Once the towers are built, test their stability by lightly shaking the surface or blowing on them to see if they hold up.
5. Discuss what worked or didn't work in building the towers. Highlight creative approaches and problem-solving efforts.
6. Ensure all materials are collected and the area is clean. Reflect on how balance and stability played a role in building the towers.

Why It's Great:
- Encourages creativity and experimentation through hands-on problem-solving.
- Teaches the basic principles of balance and stability in structure.
- Promotes teamwork and communication when working together.

Remember:
- Trial and error is key to learning; encourage children to adjust their designs.
- Make sure all materials are collected to keep the area clean.
- Celebrate all efforts, whether the tower stands tall or falls, as part of the learning process.

NOTES

Hello, December

12   DECEMBER

December is a time of quiet and reflection as nature settles into the colder months. Frost covers the landscape, and the short days bathe the world in soft golden light during early mornings and late afternoons. Mist and fog add a sense of mystery, making forests feel dreamlike, and with the foliage gone, hidden details like stone walls and ancient paths become more visible.

In Scottish tradition, December is marked by the winter solstice, a time to celebrate light returning. Ancient practices like bringing holly and ivy indoors symbolise life's endurance through winter, and simple acts like gathering evergreen branches connect us to these traditions.

Despite the cold, December holds quiet wonders. Whether it's the golden light of a frosty morning, the stillness of frozen lochs, or the sight of a snow bunting, winter's beauty awaits those who venture outside. Bundle up, step into nature, and embrace the peacefulness this month offers.

12 THE MONTH

5th	World Soil Day
6th	Tree Dressing Day
7th	World Aviation Day
11th	International Mountain Day
14th (ends 22nd)	Hannukah
21st	National Robin Day
	Winter Solstice
25th	Christmas Day
31st	Hogmannay

Could Do This Month...

- ♡ _____
- ♡ _____
- ♡ _____
- ♡ _____
- ♡ _____
- ♡ _____
- ♡ _____

12 GARDENING

As the year comes to a close, my garden is slowly winding down, signalling the end of the growing season. There's a sense of calm as the plants have done their work, and now it's my turn to make sure everything is in order. I can take the time to tidy up, ensuring the garden is neat and ready for its winter slumber. I'll clear away any debris, organise my tools, and make sure everything is prepared for a restful break over Christmas. There's something satisfying about seeing the garden ready for its "wee nap", knowing it's prepped for a fresh start in the new year.

However, there's still a final treat if I've planned well and planted some winter crops earlier in the year. Sprouts, leeks, parsnips, swedes, salad greens, and potatoes might be ready for harvesting, just in time for Christmas. It's a wonderful feeling to head out to the garden on a crisp winter day, dig up fresh vegetables, and know they'll be part of a festive feast. Harvesting these hearty vegetables is a rewarding way to close out the gardening season, as they bring a homegrown touch to Christmas dinner. Whether it's the earthy flavour of roasted parsnips and swede or the crunch of a winter salad, these crops are a reminder of the garden's ongoing cycle, even as it rests.

12 NIGHT SKY

Full Moon – December 4, 2025
This Full Moon is known as the Cold Moon. It will be at perigee, making it a supermoon, appearing slightly larger and brighter than usual. The Moon will rise around sunset and set around sunrise, making it visible for much of the night.

Geminid Meteor Shower – December 14, 2025
One of the most spectacular meteor showers of the year, the Geminids will peak on this night, potentially producing up to 120 meteors per hour. The meteors will be visible throughout the night, best seen in dark skies after midnight.

Ursid Meteor Shower – December 22, 2025
Although a smaller meteor shower, the Ursids will still offer a decent show, with about 5-10 meteors per hour. The best time to observe them will be after midnight

The Moon Phases
Full Moon	4th December
Last Quarter	11th December
New Moon	20th December
First Quarter	27th December

12 WILDLIFE

Frozen ponds and lochs in December reflect the pale winter sky, creating a peaceful, mirror-like effect. Ducks glide across icy waters, and though the ice may not be thick enough to walk on, it's a beautiful sight that invites exploration of Scotland's lochs. For winter enthusiasts, outdoor curling or skating on frozen rinks offers a fun way to enjoy the season.

In the uplands, snow buntings and ptarmigans blend into the snowy landscape with their white plumage, making winter hikes a special opportunity to spot these resilient birds. Scotland's coasts transform in December, with wild seas and dramatic waves, offering stunning views and, if lucky, the chance to see orcas.

Mountain hares, turning white in winter, are easier to spot in places like the Cairngorms and Highlands, while white-tailed eagles soar over coastal areas such as Mull and Skye. Waxwings, winter visitors from Scandinavia, can be seen feeding on berries in woodlands and parks, adding a splash of colour to the winter landscape.

12 GARDEN LIFE

In December, your Scottish garden settles into a quieter phase as wildlife adapts to the winter cold. Birds like robins, wrens, and blackbirds become regular visitors to feeders, relying on high-energy foods like fat balls, seeds, and mealworms to help them through the shorter days. These regulars might be joined by flocks of winter-visiting birds, such as redwings and fieldfares, which feast on berries from holly or other fruit-bearing shrubs. Their presence adds a welcome splash of colour and activity to the garden during the stillness of winter.

Hedgehogs will usually be hibernating at this time, nestled into sheltered spots. Providing undisturbed areas like log piles, leaf piles, or purpose-built hedgehog homes can make a big difference, giving them a safe space to sleep through the cold months. If you're fortunate enough to have these small garden visitors, ensuring they aren't disturbed is key to their survival during hibernation.

Insects, for the most part, are dormant as well. However, on particularly mild winter days, you might still spot hardy species, like the occasional bumblebee or winter moth, making a brief appearance. Though less active, these insects play a vital role in the ecosystem, even in winter.

12 COOKING

Campfire Hot Chocolate

Ingredients:
500ml milk (or plant-based milk)
2 tbsp cocoa powder (or hot chocolate mix)
2 tbsp sugar (optional)
50g dark chocolate, chopped (optional)
A pinch of salt
Marshmallows and whipped cream (optional)

Instructions:
1. Heat the milk in a pot over a campfire or stove, stirring occasionally. Avoid boiling.
2. Whisk in the cocoa powder, sugar, and salt until fully dissolved.
3. For extra richness, stir in the chopped dark chocolate until melted.
4. Pour into mugs and top with toasted marshmallows or whipped cream, if desired.

12 THE SEA

Date		High Water Morning		High Water Afternoon		Low Water Morning		Low Water Afternoon	
		Time	m	Time	m	Time	m	Time	m
1	M	10 49	4.3	22 51	4.5	04 00	1.5	16 26	1.9
2	TU	11 42	4.5	23 49	4.8	04 56	1.3	17 19	1.6
3	W			12 30	4.8	05 47	1.1	18 11	1.3
4	TH ○	00 42	5.0	13 15	4.9	06 36	1.0	18 59	1.1
5	F	01 33	5.1	13 59	5.0	07 24	1.0	19 49	0.9
6	SA	02 24	5.2	14 43	5.1	08 12	1.1	20 40	0.8
7	SU	03 15	5.1	15 28	5.0	09 00	1.3	21 32	0.9
8	M	04 10	4.9	16 17	4.9	09 47	1.5	22 25	1.0
9	TU	05 05	4.7	17 09	4.7	10 37	1.7	23 22	1.1
10	W	06 02	4.4	18 05	4.6	11 30	1.9		
11	TH ☾	06 59	4.1	19 04	4.4	00 19	1.3	12 28	2.1
12	F	08 01	4.0	20 08	4.2	01 19	1.5	13 30	2.3
13	SA	09 04	3.9	21 15	4.1	02 21	1.7	14 37	2.3
14	SU	10 09	3.9	22 21	4.1	03 25	1.8	15 47	2.3
15	M	11 06	4.0	23 20	4.1	04 24	1.8	16 48	2.1
16	TU	11 53	4.1			05 13	1.8	17 37	2.0
17	W	00 10	4.2	12 33	4.3	05 55	1.7	18 19	1.8
18	TH	00 53	4.3	13 09	4.4	06 32	1.7	18 57	1.7
19	F	01 33	4.4	13 43	4.5	07 08	1.7	19 33	1.5
20	SA ●	02 10	4.4	14 15	4.6	07 42	1.6	20 08	1.4
21	SU	02 46	4.5	14 48	4.7	08 16	1.6	20 44	1.4
22	M	03 21	4.5	15 20	4.7	08 51	1.6	21 20	1.3
23	TU	03 58	4.4	15 55	4.7	09 26	1.6	21 58	1.3
24	W	04 36	4.3	16 31	4.6	10 04	1.7	22 38	1.4
25	TH	05 18	4.3	17 13	4.5	10 44	1.8	23 22	1.4
26	F	06 03	4.2	17 58	4.4	11 29	1.9		
27	SA ☽	06 56	4.1	18 52	4.4	00 10	1.5	12 22	2.0
28	SU	07 54	4.0	19 55	4.3	01 07	1.5	13 25	2.0
29	M	08 58	4.0	21 04	4.3	02 10	1.6	14 36	2.0
30	TU	10 05	4.1	22 16	4.4	03 15	1.6	15 46	1.9
31	W	11 11	4.3	23 28	4.5	04 23	1.6	16 56	1.7

HEIGHTS ABOVE CHART DATUM

Time Zone UT(GMT)

12   SCAVENGER

While on a walk, participants will observe their surroundings and find natural items that are either bigger or smaller than different parts of their body.

Head out on a nature walk, encouraging participants to explore as they go. No need for a list—just use their eyes and imagination!

As you walk, ask participants to find things in nature that are:
- Smaller than their hand.
- Bigger than their foot.
- Smaller than their head.
- Bigger than they are.
- Smaller than their pinky finger.

Encourage them to stop and point out anything interesting they notice, whether it's a tiny pebble or a large tree. Compare the sizes as you go, using body parts like their hands, feet, or even their whole self.

As you walk, have conversations about their discoveries. Ask:
- What's the smallest thing you can find?
- Can you find something bigger than you?

SOIL ANALYSIS

Objective:
Explore soil composition and texture through hands-on observation and simple experiments.

What You'll Need:
Spade
Water
Glass jar
Laundry detergent
Measuring tools
Soil texture infographic

Instructions:
1. Soil Collection (10 minutes):
   Dig a small hole in the playground and collect soil, removing debris and rocks. Discuss its appearance and feel—look for sand, different colours, and how it holds together in your hand.
2. Water and Soil Test (10 minutes):
   Add water to the soil and try rolling it into a ball. If it sticks, the soil may contain clay.
3. Impact Test (5 minutes):
   Throw the soil balls at a hard surface. Observe if they bounce, crumble, or splatter, and discuss what this tells you about the soil.
4. Soil Jar Test (15 minutes):
   Collect fresh soil, fill a jar ¼ full with soil, add water

and detergent, and shake for 5 minutes. Let it settle for 48 hours to separate into layers of sand, silt, and clay.
5. Observation and Measurement (after 48 hours): Measure each layer, calculate percentages, and use the infographic to determine the soil texture.

Why It's Great:
- Engages students in hands-on learning.
- Teaches soil composition in a simple, interactive way.

Remember:
- Observe the soil closely.
- Trial and error is part of learning.
- Teamwork is key during experiments.

WINTER DOOR HANGING

Objective:
Create a festive winter door hanging using natural materials collected outdoors.

What You'll Need:
3 twigs
Festive foliage (leaves, berries, etc.)
String or wool
Florist wire (optional)

Instructions:
1. Go for a walk and collect 3 twigs and some festive foliage. Make sure to leave enough berries for the birds.
2. Shape the frame. Lay the twigs in a triangle shape (or any shape you like) for a simple, impactful design.
3. Secure the twigs. Tie the twigs together at each corner using wool or yarn, wrapping it around several times for stability. Secure with a knot.
4. Decorate the frame by attaching foliage in a way that appeals to you. Use string or florist wire to secure the greenery.

5. Add a loop of string to the top and find the perfect spot to hang your festive door decoration.

Why It's Great:
- Encourages creativity with natural materials.
- Simple, eco-friendly, and festive.
- Provides an opportunity to explore outdoors.

Remember:
- Be mindful of nature—leave enough berries for the birds.
- Personalise your design; there's no wrong way to create!

WINTER WALL HANGING

Objective:
Create a simple and festive winter hanging decoration using natural materials.

What You'll Need:
A twig or stick
Festive foliage (leaves, berries, etc.)
String or wool

Instructions:
1. Collect a twig and some festive foliage, like berries and leaves. Remember to leave enough berries for the birds.
2. Lay out your collected items underneath the stick to see what looks good. Arrange the foliage and natural finds in any way that appeals to you.
3. Use yarn or string to attach one end of each piece of foliage to the stick. Be creative—there's no set way to do it!
4. Tie a loop of string to each end of the stick so you can hang your decoration wherever you choose.

Why It's Great:

- Simple, eco-friendly, and creative.
- Encourages outdoor exploration and creativity with natural materials.

Remember:
- Leave plenty of berries for the birds.
- Have fun with your design—there's no right or wrong way to create your hanging!

NATURAL STAR

Objective:
Create a natural star using twigs collected from nature.

What You'll Need:
6 twigs (roughly the same length)
String or wool
Scissors
Optional: florist wire

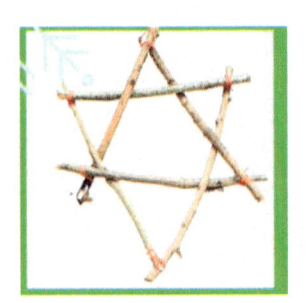

Instructions:
1. Go for a walk. Collect 6 twigs that are roughly the same length.
2. Start the base. Bind the ends of two twigs together with string or wool.
3. Form a triangle. Add the third twig, binding its ends to the first two twigs, forming a triangle shape.
4. Weave the next twig. Take the fourth twig and weave it between two sides of the triangle, binding it at the ends.
5. Add the next twig. Weave the fifth twig through and bind both ends together with the existing structure.
6. Finish and attach the hanger. Weave the final twig in, securing it at both ends. Attach a loop of string at the top to hang your natural star.

Why It's Great:
- Encourages creativity and outdoor exploration.
- Simple, eco-friendly, and festive.
- Helps develop fine motor skills by weaving and binding.

Remember:
- Use strong knots to keep your star stable.
- Have fun with the process—there's no wrong way to create your star!

PINECONE TREE

Objective:
Create a festive pinecone decoration using simple materials.

What You'll Need:
Pinecones (1 or more)
Green poster paint
Glitter or salt
Tiny pom poms
PVA glue (optional)
String (optional, for hanging)

Instructions:
1. Go for a walk and collect a pinecone or two—larger ones work well, but smaller ones are great too.
2. Use green poster paint to cover the pinecones. The brighter the paint, the more festive!
3. While the paint is still wet, sprinkle glitter or salt over the pinecones to create a shimmering effect. Allow them to dry completely.
4. Squeeze tiny pom poms into the gaps between the scales of the pinecone. Use a bit of PVA glue if needed to keep them secure.
5. Find a special spot to place your decorated pine cone, or tie a string around the top to hang it as a festive ornament.

Why It's Great:
- Simple and fun festive craft using natural materials.
- Encourages creativity with painting and decorating.

Remember:
- You can mix and match colours with your pom poms and glitter.
- Let the paint dry completely before handling or hanging your pinecone.

NOTES

FIND OUT MORE

I hope you have enjoyed this and it has inspired you to get outdoors more. Did you know we have a full website of ideas for you?

I would love for you to continue your outdoor journey with me. You can find free resources, our blog and even our podcast on our website.

Check it out by following the QR code below or heading right over to:

www.loveoutdoorlearning.com

And, if you want ideas direct to your inbox sign up for our newsletter at: